The
Indian
Book

The Indian Book

The 1980 Childcraft Annual

An annual supplement to
Childcraft—The How and Why Library

World Book–Childcraft International, Inc.

A subsidiary of The Scott & Fetzer Company

Chicago London Paris Sydney Tokyo Toronto

Contents

Preface

This book is about the Indians of North and South America. In it, you will find out who these people are and where they came from. You will see how they lived before the people of Europe came to their lands. Finally, you will learn something of what it is like to be an Indian today.

The people Columbus called "Indians" were—and are—many very different groups of people. They had hundreds of languages, wore different kinds of clothing, and ate different kinds of food. Some lived in tepees and some in wooden houses. And they had many different beliefs.

The thirteen tribes in this book show these many differences. Life for a Tlingit boy on the western coast of Canada was not at all like that of a Hopi girl in the Southwestern part of the United States, or an Aztec boy in Mexico, or an Inca girl in the Andes Mountains of Peru. For *how* each Indian group lived depended very much upon *where* it lived.

So come, find out what it was like to be an Indian child hundreds of years ago—before these ways of life changed forever.

The Ancestors of the Indians

Who *are* the American Indians? Have they always lived in North and South America? If not, where did they come from?

Long ago, there were no people at all in North or South America. But there were people in other parts of the world. And about thirty thousand years ago, some wandering hunters from Asia entered what is now Alaska. They were the first people in North America. Others followed them.

Slowly, over thousands of years, the descendants of these hunters spread through North America. In time, they got all the way to the very tip of South America.

Some of these people lived mainly by hunting. Others learned to grow plants for food. Some built rich civilizations, with great cities and beautiful works of art. These hunters, farmers, artists, and builders were the ancestors of the people Christopher Columbus met when he arrived in 1492.

Columbus thought he had landed in a part of Asia known as the Indies. Because of this he called the people he met "Indians." And this is the name they have been known by ever since.

The first Americans

The short summer was over. The fierce winter was beginning. Tiny, whirling flakes of snow filled the dark-gray sky. Already, frost coated the brittle, yellow grass of the plain.

Across this plain trudged a group of men, women, and children. They all wore clothes made of furry animal skins—thick boots, heavy, long pants, and hooded jackets. All of the men carried spears that had points made of chipped stone.

Most of the people had bundles strapped to their backs. Some carried firewood. Others had large animal-skin bags filled with dried meat. And some packed rolled-up animal skins that were used to make rough shelters.

These people were wandering hunters. They followed the herds of caribou, or wild reindeer, that moved back and forth over the plain. From the caribou, they got meat, skins for tents and clothing, and bones for tools. They depended on the caribou for almost everything they needed.

This small band of hunters was following a caribou herd eastward. They had no idea they were headed for a place no human had ever seen. They were moving from Asia into Alaska. They were the first people to reach the continent now called North America.

All this took place about thirty thousand years ago. At that time, the world was in the cold, white grip of an Ice Age. A lot of the ocean water had become huge mountains of ice called glaciers. These glaciers covered large areas of the earth. With so much water gone from it, the ocean was much lower than it is now.

The plain upon which the caribou hunters walked into North America was actually part of the sea-bottom. This "land bridge," nearly a thousand miles (1,600 kilometers) wide, connected Asia with Alaska. Today, it is under water. But until about ten thousand years ago, the land was often above water. And during many thousands of years, groups of people crossed into Alaska.

At times, the way out of Alaska was blocked by huge glaciers. But during warm periods, the ice barriers melted. Ways out of Alaska opened up. Groups of people moved south and east. By about twenty thousand years ago, there were people living in many parts of North America. By at least eight thousand years ago, people had found their way to the southern tip of South America.

Many thousands of years ago, Asia and Alaska were joined together by a wide strip of land. About thirty thousand years ago, the ancestors of the American Indians began crossing this land bridge from Asia into North America.

The mighty hunters

The prehistoric people living in North America thousands of years ago lived in a land of plenty. Animals by the thousands roamed the huge forests and great plains. There were herds of the big, furry elephants we call mammoths and mastodons. There were huge bison and odd-looking camels. And there were deer, bear, and dozens of other big animals.

The people who lived among these animals still lived by hunting, just as their ancestors had. Their weapons were spears with points of chipped stone. But with only these weapons, prehistoric Americans hunted even the biggest of all animals, the mastodon and mammoth. We know this because people have found stone spearpoints in skeletons of these animals—the points of the spears that killed them!

Sometimes the hunters may have ambushed a mammoth when it was alone, perhaps when it came to drink at a stream. They may have thrown their spears at it, wounding it in many places. Or, perhaps they set fires or waved torches to frighten it.

The hunters wanted to force the mammoth into the stream, so that the big creature's feet would sink into the muddy bottom. Then, as the trapped mammoth struggled in rage and terror, some men thrust spears at it. Others threw rocks. Soon, the mammoth would grow weak and die.

Of course, the hunters were often in danger. Sometimes, some of them must have been hurt or killed by the sharp tusks and trampling feet of the giant elephants!

Prehistoric Americans often hunted herds of bison. They would trail a herd until it was near the edge of a cliff or deep ravine. Then the hunters would throw spears and wave and shout to frighten the animals and make them stampede toward the edge. Scores of the big animals would fall to the bottom of the cliff, killing themselves or breaking bones so they couldn't move. Then the hunters would butcher them.

These people were truly mighty hunters. Many scientists think they were such good hunters that they may have killed all the mastodons and mammoths that roamed North America ten thousand years ago!

These are the stone points of Indian spears. They were found in Arizona, with the bones of a huge mammoth. Indian hunters killed the animal with spears about twelve thousand years ago.

The first farmers

By about ten thousand years ago, North America was changing. The great glaciers were nearly gone. The climate was warmer and drier. Deserts began to appear in the western part of the continent. The great mastodons, mammoths, and many other kinds of creatures were nearly all gone.

People learned how to grow corn, or maize, about five thousand years ago. The first corn looked like this.

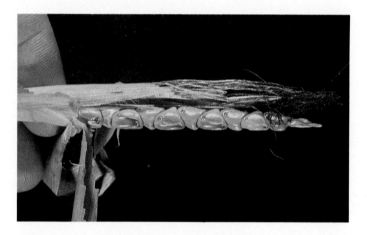

These changes meant new ways of life for many prehistoric Americans. Many small animals roamed the land, but the hunting was not as easy as it had been. People began to depend more on plants for food. They ate nuts and the seeds of grasses and other plants. They learned which plants had roots that were good to eat. They discovered where they could find ripe berries and other fruits at different times of the year.

But it takes a lot of plant food to feed even a few people. So those prehistoric Americans who existed mostly by gathering plant food lived in small groups. And they had to keep moving. Once the plant food in a place was eaten up, the people had to go to another place where there was more food.

Some of these people learned that seeds put into the ground sprout into new plants. They began to plant seeds in new places. And they pulled up unwanted plants to make room for those they wanted. By about five thousand years ago, people in what is now Mexico had become the first American farmers. They grew regular crops of corn (maize), beans, squash, red peppers, and avocados. But the plants they grew were much smaller than the same kinds that farmers grow today.

Other prehistoric people learned about this way of growing food where it was wanted, instead of moving around to look for it. People in many places became farmers. Now that they could stay in one place, these people began to build villages and towns.

The Mound Builders

In the state of Wisconsin there is what looks like a long, low mound of earth. But if you stand on top of the mound, you can see that it is shaped like a flying goose. The wings spread out on each side and a long neck stretches out in front.

In Ohio, there is a mound shaped like an enormous snake. This low, winding mound is some thirteen hundred feet (396 meters) long. And in Illinois, a flat-topped mound rises a hundred feet (30 m) above the plain.

There are thousands and thousands of mounds, of all shapes and sizes, throughout the eastern half of the United States. Some look like birds and animals. Some are shaped like people. Others are cone-shaped. And many look like a pyramid with a flat top.

To make such mounds, a great many people worked for months and even years. Using sticks, large clamshells, and the bones of animals, they dug up tons of dirt. In bags made of animal skin, or in woven baskets, they carried the dirt to where they wanted to build a mound.

But when, and why, did people build these mounds? The earliest mounds were built about three thousand years ago, in what are now the states of Ohio and Kentucky. The people used these small, dome-shaped mounds as graves in which to bury their dead. Valuable objects that may have belonged to the dead people—stone pipes, pottery, jewelry, little carved statues, and other things—were buried with them.

Most of the people in the United States and

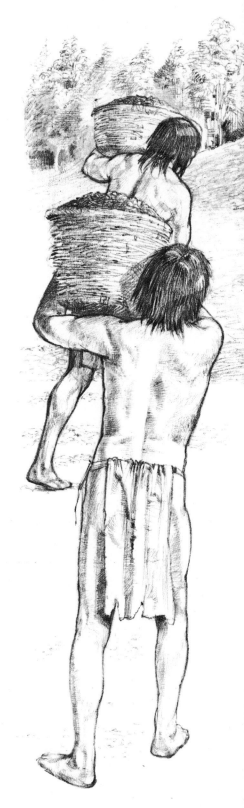

The Mound Builders made their mounds by piling up dirt to form a special shape. The Great Serpent Mound, shown below, may have taken hundreds of people years to build.

The Great Serpent Mound is in Ohio.

This pipe, shaped like a man, was made by Mound Builders. They often buried pipes and other things in their mounds.

Canada three thousand years ago were wandering hunters. But not the early Mound Builders. They lived in small villages. They had round houses with cone-shaped roofs. These people were artists and skillful pottery makers. We don't know if they grew crops, but they did weave cloth from bark.

The mound-building idea soon began to spread. After a time, people living in what are now Ohio and Illinois began to build large cone-shaped burial mounds. These mounds had log tombs inside them. People buried in the tombs seem to have been important people, such as chiefs.

These new Mound Builders were fine artists. They made ornaments of copper, jewelry of pearls from river shellfish, and little, lifelike clay statues of people. They were also great traders. They often traveled great distances to get the special materials they wanted. Some of the things they used came from as far away as the Gulf of Mexico and the Rocky Mountains. Because of these people, mound-building spread through the North, East, and South.

At about the same time, other people in

Ohio, northern Illinois, southern Wisconsin, and eastern Iowa built many mounds of a very different kind. The mounds they built are shaped like animals, birds, and people. No one knows exactly when any of these mounds were made, or who made them.

About thirteen hundred years ago, people who lived in what is now the southern part of the United States began to build a new kind of mound. It was a broad, flat-topped hill with sloping sides—like a pyramid with the top half cut off. A row of steps, made of logs, ran up one side of the mound. And instead of burying their dead in the mound, the people built a temple on the flat top.

We don't know what sort of religion the temple mounds were used for. But many people must have liked it, because the idea of temple mounds spread northward.

About a thousand years ago, people in southern Illinois built a large temple mound near the Mississippi River. This mound is now called Monk's Mound. It is the largest earthwork in the world. It stands about one hundred feet (30 m) high. At its base, it is bigger around than the Great Pyramid of Egypt. When the mound was built, it was the center of a city of some thirty thousand people. Today, only the mound is left.

Mound building was carried on for more than two thousand years. But by the time the Spanish explorers came to America in the early 1500's, all mound building had stopped. Many Indian tribes living in the south—the Creek, Cherokee, Natchez, and others—still used old temple mounds. But no new mounds of any kind were being built.

The Cliff Dwellers

The land where the states of Utah, Colorado, Arizona, and New Mexico come together is desert. Prehistoric people lived in this area more than two thousand years ago. These people lived in small groups, in caves in the sides of cliffs or in crude huts made with the branches of desert shrubs. They ate seeds of wild plants and any desert animals they could kill.

About eighteen hundred years ago, these people learned to grow corn. To store dried corn, they dug pits in the floors of caves. This may have given them the idea for a different kind of house. To make this new house, they first dug a pit in the ground. They used poles to make a roof over the pit. Finally they plastered the roof with clay.

The door to the house was an opening in the roof. To get into the house, people climbed down a ladder. When they were inside, sitting on the floor, they were actually underground. Usually, the people built these houses close to a cliff wall.

Hundreds of years went by. The people's way of building houses changed. Now they made a rectangle-shaped framework of wooden poles or stone, all above ground. They covered the framework with clay. They built their houses so that the wall of one house was also the wall of another house. The people still kept some of the old underground pit houses. But these became special places used for religious ceremonies.

By about eight hundred years ago, the communities of these desert people had changed again. Now there were hundreds of houses forming tall towers and great square buildings, all joined together. Such places looked like vast castles nestled against the walls of cliffs. But even these great "cities" had a number of underground pit houses for special ceremonies.

The people who lived in these marvelous cliff dwellings had a high standard of living. They grew corn and other crops in nearby fields. They wove cloth for their clothes. And they made fine pottery decorated with beautiful designs.

Today, you can see the ruins of old cliff dwellings, standing silent and empty, in many parts of the southwest. What could have happened to the Cliff Dwellers?

These are the ruins of a Cliff Dweller village. They are nearly a thousand years old. Called Cliff Palace, the ruins are in Mesa Verde National Park, Colorado.

About seven hundred years ago, there was a long dry period. The southwest desert country never gets very much rain, but for more than twenty years there was almost no rain at all. Unable to raise crops, the people abandoned many communities. There may have been other reasons as well.

Those people were the ancestors of the Hopi and Taos Indians of today. The Hopi and Taos people still make some of their houses out of stone and clay, as did their ancestors. They still have underground pit houses, called kivas (KEE vuhs). The kivas are both clubhouses for men and places where special religious ceremonies are held, just as they were a thousand years ago.

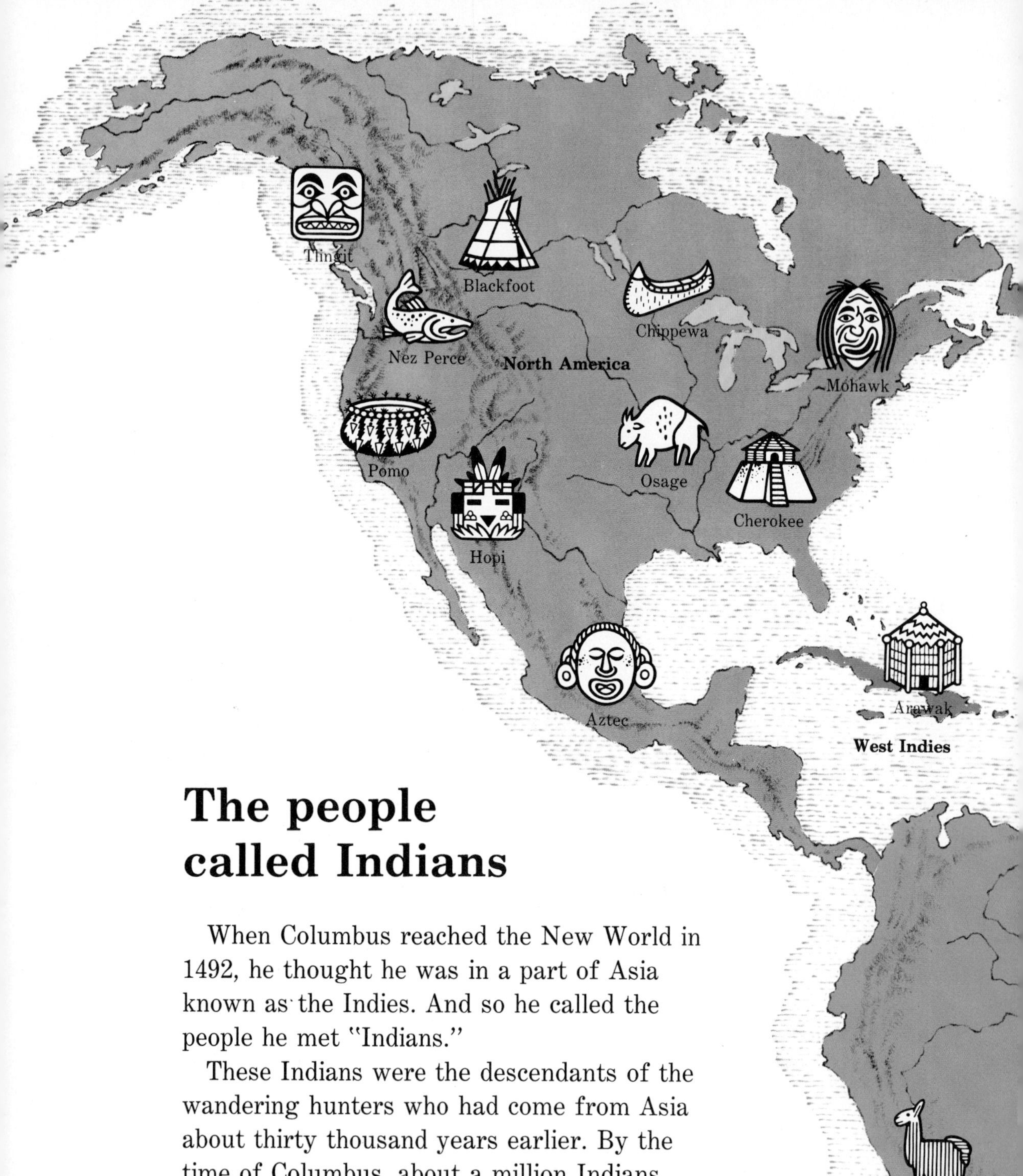

Tlingit

Blackfoot

Nez Perce

Chippewa

North America

Mohawk

Pomo

Osage

Cherokee

Hopi

Aztec

Arawak

West Indies

Inca

The people called Indians

When Columbus reached the New World in 1492, he thought he was in a part of Asia known as the Indies. And so he called the people he met "Indians."

These Indians were the descendants of the wandering hunters who had come from Asia about thirty thousand years earlier. By the time of Columbus, about a million Indians lived in what are now the United States, Canada, and Alaska. Another seven million or so lived in Mexico, Central America, and the Caribbean. And at least ten million lived in South America.

The many groups, or tribes, often had very different ways of life and different beliefs.

Some groups lived in forests and some on vast plains. Others lived in the desert or on the seacoast. Some lived much as their ancestors had, getting their food by hunting animals and gathering wild plants. Others were farmers who grew most of their food. Some were skillful sailors and fishermen.

Some groups lived in tiny villages, others in large cities. Some made their houses of animal skins, some had houses of stone, and still others had wooden houses. Some lived in small bands and chose their leaders. Others lived in huge empires and were ruled by kings.

In North America alone, the people spoke more than two hundred different languages. Often, the people of one group, or "tribe," did not understand the language of another tribe that lived near them.

We call all these people "Indians," which makes them seem very much alike. But, as you will see, they were—and still are—very different from one another.

South America

Yawalapiti

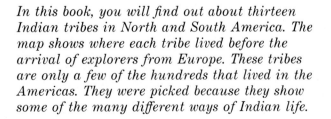

In this book, you will find out about thirteen Indian tribes in North and South America. The map shows where each tribe lived before the arrival of explorers from Europe. These tribes are only a few of the hundreds that lived in the Americas. They were picked because they show some of the many different ways of Indian life.

The Chippewa

People of the Northern Woodlands

The Chippewa, also called Ojibwa, were one
of the largest Indian tribes north of Mexico.
They lived in what is now northern Wisconsin
and Minnesota, and part of Ontario, Canada.
Towering oak, birch, and maple trees covered
their land.

The Chippewa moved through the forest in
bands of three or four hundred people. Each
band had its own part of the forest in which
to hunt and gather plant food. There was no
chief of the whole tribe. Each band had its
own leader. When a leader died, his son
became the new leader.

Many rivers ran through the land of the
Chippewa. And many small lakes, as well as
the great lake now called Lake Superior, lay
in their country. So the Chippewa often
traveled from place to place by water, in
canoes made of birchbark.

A number of other tribes lived in the forest
near the Chippewa. Among these were the
Menominee, Sauk, Fox, Winnebago, and
Kickapoo. To the west, where the forest
ended and the plains began, lived the Cree
and the Dakota, or Sioux, people.

Life in the forest

Grasshopper walked through the forest with her family and the other people who belonged to the band led by Old Man. It was a bright, hot summer day, but the forest was cool and dim. The leafy branches of the trees shut out much of the sunlight.

There were more than two hundred people in Old Man's band—men, women, and children of all ages. They were part of the great tribe of people who called themselves Anishinabe (Ay-nihsh-ihn-ay-beh), meaning "First Men." There were many bands of the First Men in other parts of the forest.

The people of Old Man's band walked quietly, in single file, one behind another. By making only a narrow path, the people let the forest and the animals know that they were only passing through, not claiming ownership. For the forest belonged to the animals—not to the Anishinabe.

Yet the forest was home to Grasshopper and her people. They moved about it freely, going from place to place. Because they depended upon the forest, the rivers, and the lakes for all their food, they never stayed in one place very long. They went wherever the hunting or fishing was best, or where wild plant food had become ripe enough to eat.

Now they were on their way to a part of the forest where they knew wild blueberries grew. They went there at about the same time every year. In fact, they called this time of year "Plenty-of-Blueberries Moon." Grasshopper licked her lips at the thought of sweet blueberries.

"Grasshopper" was not her real name. It was a nickname her father had given her. Her real name was Coming-Over-the-Hill. But no one ever called her by this name. A person's real name was a very important thing that must be kept secret.

Grasshopper had been given her real name when she was a tiny baby. An old woman who had dreamed of deer coming over a hill had given it to her. A real name could be given only by a very old person who had always been healthy. Then the child would always be healthy and would grow to be very old, too.

Just then, one of Grasshopper's little brothers strayed off the path, into the woods. One of her fathers called him back, sharply. The man who called was not her real father. He was one of her father's brothers. But Grasshopper called both of her father's brothers "father." She also called their wives "mother." And she called their children brothers and sisters. All of these people, together with her father's father and mother were Grasshopper's family.

The family had no last name. But all the men belonged to a group of related people who called themselves the Bear clan, or Bear group. All of the children belonged to the Bear clan because their fathers did. The mothers belonged to other clans, for people of the same clan never married one another. When, in time, Grasshopper married, she would join another family. Her children would belong to the clan of the man she married, such as Wolf, or Goose. But Grasshopper would always belong to the Bear clan.

Grasshopper wiggled her shoulders to ease the weight of the small bundle on her back. Everyone in the band carried a bundle. Whenever they moved to another place, they took all their belongings with them. Many of the women even carried parts of houses with them—long rolled up sheets of birchbark.

The band reached the berry patch in late afternoon. Everyone went right to work.

The women began to put up the houses. A number of dome-shaped frames made of trimmed tree branches already stood in the small clearing near the berry patch. These frames had been built years before. Now, the women unrolled the sheets of birchbark they had carried. They used these to cover the frames. While the band stayed at the berry patch, the people would sleep in these birchbark-covered huts.

The men and older boys went hunting. Grasshopper and many of the other children went to pick berries. They put the berries into square buckets made of birchbark.

Soon, the setting sun sent orange shafts of light slanting through the trees. Shadows began to fill the forest. Some of the women started fires.

To start a fire, they twirled a hard, pointed wooden stick between their hands. The point of the stick pressed against a piece of soft bark. As the point spun, it ground some of the bark to powder. The spinning end of the pointed stick and the powdered bark got hotter and hotter. Finally, the powdered bark caught fire. Quickly, the women fed the fire with twigs and leaves.

The men and boys returned from their hunt. They had managed to kill only a few birds. But they had set a number of traps. And they had found a trail used by deer. Tomorrow, they would have more time, and probably better luck. But for now, each family had a small supply of dried meat and fish—and there were plenty of blueberries.

Night fell. The cluster of fires twinkled in the darkness. Around each fire sat a family group. At Grasshopper's family fire, all of the children sat silent and wide-eyed as Grandmother told stories.

She told of the Windego, the giant who eats people. She spoke of Ba-kak, the creature that looks like a skeleton and goes about doing harm to people. She also told tales of Hare, the great spirit that had given the First Men fire and other things.

One by one, as the fires died down, the families went into their little houses to sleep. Grasshopper curled up with her brothers and

sisters on mats made of dried rushes. The
last thing she heard before she fell asleep
was the sound of an owl hooting in the
blackness of the forest.

The people of the band would stay at the
berry patch for several weeks. They would
pick all the berries they could. Many berries
would be eaten, but many would be dried for
later use. Then, the people would move to the
shore of the great lake. There they gathered
wild rice each year. They would stay there
for a time, gathering the rice and drying it.
Then they would move on to another part of
the woods.

Grasshopper's world was the great lake
and the forest that surrounded it. The huts in
the woods or by the lake weren't homes. They
were just places to sleep. The forest was
Grasshopper's home. Everything she needed
came from the forest or the lake.

Chippewa ways

If you had been a Chippewa child of long ago, you would have worn clothes made from the skin of a fawn, or young deer. Your parents would have clothes made from the skins of deer, elk, or moose. The Chippewa, like all woodland Indians, made their clothes from the skins of animals.

Your mother would have done all the work to prepare the skins. This was a long and hard task. If you had been a teen-aged girl, you'd have helped.

First, your mother would soak the skin in water for several days. Then, after wringing it out, she'd use a sharp-edged stone to scrape off all the hair.

Next, she would soak the skin overnight in water in which deer brains had been boiled. Then she'd scrape the skin again and again to get rid of the last bits of hair and fat. This also made it soft and smooth. Finally, she would tan the skin by smoking it over glowing birchbark embers. This would color

Chippewa women prepared the animal skins from which they made clothes for the family. To take off the hair and fat, a skin was put over a log and scraped with a sharp bone. The skin was then stretched tight on a frame and scraped again to make it smooth and soft.

the skin and protect it from moths. After
tanning, the skin would be soft as silk and
ready to be made into clothes.

Most of the time, you and your family
would sleep in a dome-shaped hut called a
wigwam. A wigwam was a simple framework
of poles covered with sheets of birchbark or
mats made of bulrushes. At the center of
your wigwam there would be a pit where a
fire could be made for light and cooking.
Your only furniture would be mats made of
dried, woven plant stems. You'd sit as well as
sleep on these mats.

Sometimes you might live in a larger house
with three or four other families. This kind of
house, called a wigwassawigimig, looked like
a peaked roof sitting on the ground. It was
made by placing two rows of poles in the
ground, slanted so the tops touched. The
poles were covered with bark sheets or mats.

If you'd been an older boy, you'd have
spent most of your time with the men,
hunting, trapping, and fishing for food. You'd
shoot moose, elk, and deer with arrows that
had been dipped in rattlesnake poison. You'd
shoot birds with blunt arrows that stunned
them.

To catch bears, you'd use a trap called a
deadfall. Such a trap drops a heavy log on
the bear, pinning the animal down. You'd
catch rabbits, foxes, and even deer in a trap

Chippewa women cut and peeled the poles used to make the frame for a wigwam. The men drove poles into the ground and then bent and held them while the women tied them. The women covered the frame with sheets of birchbark or mats made of plants called bulrushes.

The Chippewa caught bears in a trap called a deadfall. When the bear took the bait, the post holding up the crosspiece moved and the heavy logs fell on the animal.

called a snare. This kind of trap has a noose that tightens around the animal.

In warm weather, you might help the men catch fish in big nets made of woven bark. In winter, you'd fish through a hole in the ice.

In early spring, your band would go to a place where there were many sugar maple trees. Your father would make cuts in the tree trunks to allow the sap to drip into birchbark buckets. Then your mother would boil the sap down into maple sugar.

During the summer, you might help the women and other children pick berries. Then, in late August or early September, in the time called Wild-Rice-Gathering-Moon, you would move to the lake. There, your parents would gather the wild rice, one of your most important foods.

The Chippewa harvested wild rice from
their birchbark canoes. One person
guided the canoe. Others bent down the
stalks of rice and beat them lightly to
knock the ripe kernels into the canoe.
Kernels that fell into the water would
take root and grow into new plants.

The Chippewa used birchbark
containers such as this one to
store dried berries and rice.

Puckered moccasins

The Chippewa people called themselves *Anishinabe,* or "First Men." Other Indians called them the Ojibwa, which means "to roast until puckered up." But the name had nothing to do with food. It really meant "those whose moccasins have puckered seams."

To Europeans, *ojibwa* (oh JIHB way) sounded like *chippewa* (CHIHP uh way). So this is what Europeans called these people. Today, both names are used. But now the name *Chippewa* is usually pronounced CHIHP uh wah.

You can make a pair of puckered Chippewa moccasins for yourself. Here's how:

Materials

- felt or heavy cloth
- magic markers
- needle and thread
- pencil
- scissors
- tissue paper

Use the red outline on this page to make the pattern for your moccasins. The pattern is for a moccasin that will fit a foot $7\frac{1}{2}$ inches (18.7 centimeters) long. Your foot may be longer or shorter. For every $\frac{1}{2}$ inch (1.2 cm) longer your foot is, add $\frac{1}{2}$ inch (1.2 cm) to the top of the pattern. For every $\frac{1}{2}$ inch (1.2 cm) shorter your foot is, take $\frac{1}{2}$ inch (1.2 cm) off the top of the pattern.

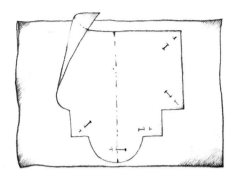

Fold a piece of tissue paper in half. Place the fold along the left edge of page 40. Use your pencil to trace the red outline onto the tissue paper. Keeping the paper folded, cut along the line you have traced.

Open the tissue-paper pattern. Pin it to a piece of felt. Following the line of the pattern, cut the shape out of the felt.

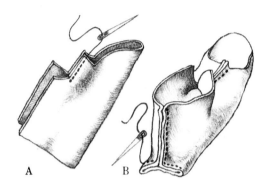

Fold the cut-out piece of felt in half. Sew the two edges together, as shown by the red dots in A.

Form the bottom of the heel into a T, as shown in B. Sew the heel together, as shown by the red dots in B.

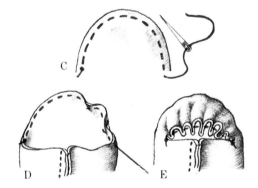

Using long stitches, sew all around the edge of the toe, as shown by the red lines in C. Do not sew anything together.

Pull the left-over thread toward you, as shown in D. When the thread is tight, the toe will pull together, as shown in E. Make a knot to hold the thread in place.

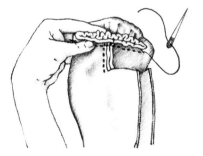

Flatten the cloth above the toe. Sew the bunched toe to the edge of the top part, as shown by the red dots.

Turn the moccasin inside out. Fold down the cloth around the ankle to make a flap. Follow the same steps to make your other moccasin. Use the magic markers to decorate your moccasins.

How Hare brought fire home

A Chippewa legend

The great god Hare was born to a young woman who lived with her mother in a wigwam in the forest. Hare's father was the west wind. When Hare was born, his mother died. His grandmother brought him up.

One day, Hare said to his grandmother, "Do any people live near us?"

"Yes," said his grandmother. "There are people living on the far shore of the lake."

"And do these people across the lake have fire?" asked Hare.

"Indeed they do," she replied.

"Then I shall go and bring back some fire for us," he said.

"Oh, you cannot do that," said his grandmother. "They keep a careful watch over their fire. There is an old man who sits at home by the fire all day long, mending a fishing net. He has two daughters who often go outside, but he never leaves the fire."

"Nevertheless, I will go," declared Hare.

When Hare came to the lake, he stood on the shore and said, "I wish this lake to freeze. I wish it to become as thick as the birchbark covering of a wigwam. Let this happen." And the lake froze.

"Now," said Hare, "let me become a small rabbit." And he was.

Then Hare started out onto the ice, which easily held his light weight. He crossed over to the far shore. There, he found a place where the water was not frozen. Hare lay down in the water and said, "Let a woman now come to get water. And let her take me home for a pet."

Almost at once, a young woman carrying a dipper came down to the water. When she saw the little rabbit, she lifted him out of the water. Tucking him inside her robe to keep him warm, she went home.

When they went into the wigwam, Hare saw the old man sitting by the fire, mending a net. The girl who had found Hare went over to her sister and whispered, "Look at the cute little rabbit I found. Isn't he nice? I hope you like him as much as I do."

Her sister whispered back, "Father will be angry if he sees it. Wait and see!"

But the girl who had found Hare took him

out of her robe and put him down by the fire
to dry. He looked so funny that the two girls
began to giggle.

"Why are you making so much noise?"
asked the old man, their father.

"Look at this cute little rabbit I found,"
said the girl.

"Beware!" exclaimed her father. "Have you
never heard of the spirits? Perhaps this is
one! Go put it back where you found it. You
were wrong to bring it here!"

But the girl said, "Oh, I like this funny
little rabbit so much! How could a little bunny
be a spirit?"

"Listen to what I tell you!" said her father,
angrily. "I am older than you, and I know
more about such things."

Then Hare thought to himself, "Let a spark
from the fire now fall upon me." And that is
what happened. A spark fell upon him and his

fur caught fire. Instantly, Hare sprang up
and dashed out of the wigwam.

"You see?" cried the girls' father. "Why
did you not listen to me! I tell you, that
rabbit is a spirit that has come to steal fire
from us!" Angrily, the old man got up and
ran after Hare.

Hare scurried to the lake and began to run
across the frozen water. The man and his
daughters saw they would never be able to
catch him. All they could do was stand and
watch him until he was out of sight.

Hare sped across the lake, his fur burning.
Soon, he saw his grandmother's wigwam
ahead. "Grandmother!" he called. "Rub this
fire off me, for I am burning up!"

His grandmother rubbed the fire off him
with some sticks. At once, the sticks began to
burn. And that is how the spirit Hare brought
fire to the land of the Chippewa.

What happened to my people

"At one time, long ago, my people—the Chippewa—were woodland Indians." As the old man spoke, he looked out across the lake to the forest on the far side. "One of your people told of our way of life, our beliefs, and our legends in a long poem, 'The Song of Hiawatha.'"

The old man paused, then went on. "That way of life was long ago. It was a dream, and now the dream is gone. For us, it ended the day we first met the whites. These people—they were French—were like us in some ways and very different in other ways. They wanted furs, and we had furs. They had all kinds of things we needed—but most of all, they had guns.

"The Chippewa have always been the bravest of warriors. Always we were ready to fight to keep what was ours." For just a moment, his eyes flashed. "With guns, we could keep the wild rice fields. And we did. We drove the Dakota, or Sioux, people onto the plains to the west. We drove the Fox south, out of Wisconsin. And when the mighty tribes of the Iroquois came at us from the east, we pushed them back.

"But in the late 1700's, white settlers came in greater and greater numbers. We had land. They wanted it. And they took it."

Then, for a moment, the old man stood straight and tall. His voice was proud as he spoke. "We held them back at first. Many tribes banded together under the Miami war chief, Little Turtle and the great Shawnee leader Tecumseh. At first, we won great victories. But we were doomed.

"An American force under General 'Mad Anthony' Wayne marched against us. The Shawnee chief Blue Jacket attacked the Americans at a place called Fallen Timbers, in what is now Ohio. They were too much for us. We thought our British friends would help. But when we fell back to one of their forts, they would not even open the gates."

The old man sat down cross-legged on the ground. "Our people were forced to give up huge amounts of land. Finally, in 1815, all the Chippewa living in the United States signed a treaty with the government. We gave up more land. Then we were sent to live in special places called reservations."

Speaking rather slowly, the old man said, "Today, there are about thirty thousand Chippewa. We live in Michigan, Wisconsin, Minnesota, and Ontario, Canada.

"Some of us live on reservations. We are poor, for there is little work. But," and he smiled, "we harvest almost all of the wild rice eaten in this country. Others, especially the young, live and work in towns and cities, just like our white brothers."

For a time, the old man said nothing. Then he spoke. And there was strength in his voice. "Our pride was almost destroyed. But a tiny spark was left. Now that spark has caught fire. We are learning to live in your world. But we are trying to keep what was best in our world."

This Chippewa woman is harvesting wild rice the same way her people did long ago. Today, most of the wild rice sold in stores is gathered by the Chippewa.

The Mohawk

People of the Longhouse

The Mohawk lived in what is now upper New York State and a bit of Canada. Their villages stood in clearings in the forest that covered the land. They had large houses, called longhouses, in which a number of families lived. The men hunted, fished, and made war. The women grew corn, beans, and squash outside the village.

Four other tribes, the Oneida, Onondaga, Cayuga, and Seneca, lived near the Mohawk. All five tribes spoke the same basic language and lived in much the same way. Long ago, these five tribes had joined together to form a strong group. They called their group by a name meaning, "we are of the longhouse."

Their enemies, the Algonquin Indians, called all the people of the longhouse by a name meaning "poisonous snakes." To French explorers, the Algonquin word sounded like Iroquois (IHR uh kwoy). We still know them by this name.

Of all the Iroquois tribes, the Mohawk were the most feared and hated. They tortured and even ate captives. It was their enemies who gave them the name Mohawk, meaning "eaters of men."

Life in a Mohawk village

It was mid-morning. For the people living in the longhouse, it was time for the main meal of the day. The men had just eaten and left. Now the women and children would have their turn.

Bright Sky sat by the fire, gobbling the corn soup his mother had given him. He ate with a large wooden spoon that had a deep bowl. The soup was the only hot food he would have during the day. His evening meal would probably be cold boiled corn.

Bright Sky's home, the longhouse, was like a long hall. There were a dozen such longhouses in the village. This was a village of the people who called themselves "The People of the Place of Flint." Their enemies, who feared and hated them, called them Mohawk, meaning "eaters of men."

The People of the Place of Flint were one of the five tribes that had joined together to form a group called the Five Nations, or the League of the Iroquois. These five tribes—the Seneca, Cayuga, Onondaga, Oneida, and Mohawk—thought of themselves as living in one great longhouse.

The Seneca, in the west, were "Keepers of the Western Door" of the longhouse. In the center were the Onondaga, "Keepers of the Wampum Belts." The Mohawk, or People of the Place of Flint, were "Keepers of the Eastern Door."

As Bright Sky sat eating in the longhouse, he thought of these things. He also thought of his family. He, his baby sister, and his mother and father were a "fireside family." All the other people living in the longhouse made up his "longhouse family." It was this group that was most important to him.

The head of the longhouse family was his grandmother—his mother's mother. She was the oldest woman of the family. Grandmother had two daughters living in the longhouse. And grandmother's sister had a daughter and a son who lived there. All three of the daughters were married and had children. All of these people made up Bright Sky's longhouse family. He called all the children his brothers and sisters.

Bright Sky's grandfather and father, as well as the husbands of the other women, lived in the longhouse. But they were not part of this longhouse family. They belonged to other longhouse families—the longhouses where their mothers and sisters lived. When Bright Sky grew up and married, he would move into the longhouse of his wife's family. Even so, he would still belong to his mother's family in the longhouse where he now lived.

Bright Sky began to wonder what his father was doing now. Two suns ago, his father and many of the other men had gone off with a war party. They had gone to raid a village of the enemy people called Hatirontaks or "tree-bark eaters."

Bright Sky remembered the excitement as the war party formed. The loud whoops of Fish Carrier, who was war chief, told the village that war had been decided on. Fish Carrier went to the war post, a wooden post that stood near the center of the village. He

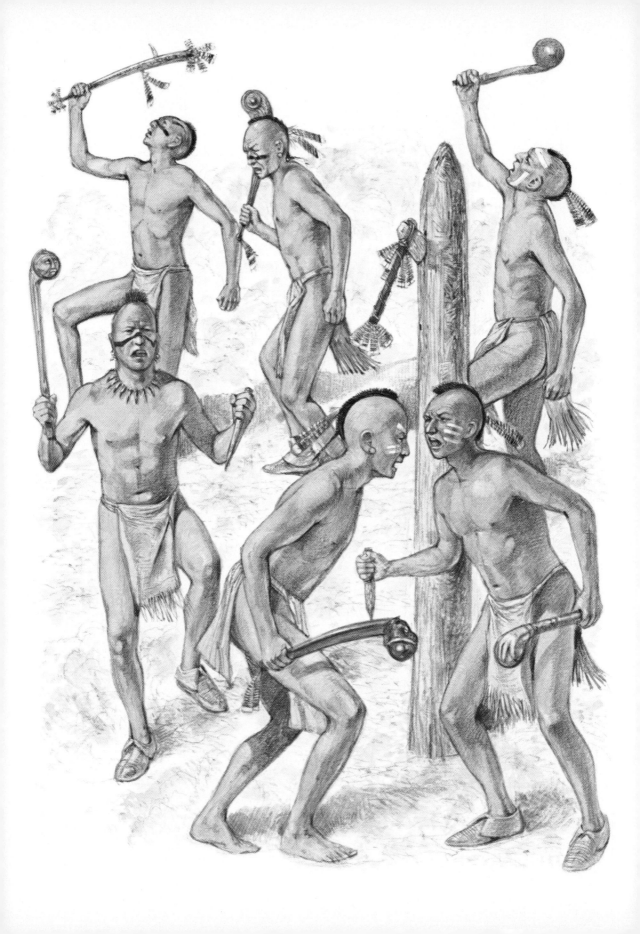

struck the post with a red-painted hatchet. The hatchet was still there, its stone head stuck in the post. It would stay there until the men returned.

Fish Carrier then began to dance. One by one, most of the young men joined in the dance. This showed their willingness to go to war. Quickly, the women brought food for the warriors—dried corn that had been ground to powder and mixed with maple sugar. The men loaded the food into bear-skin pouches, seized their bows, hatchets, and clubs, and left at once. That had been many days ago.

Bright Sky wished he were old enough to go with the war party! War was the way a man of the People of the Place of Flint proved himself worthy. It was the way to gain honor and glory. Only two moons ago, in early summer, another war party had gone on a raid. They had brought back many prisoners. All warriors had been praised and honored! Bright Sky remembered just what had happened.

First, the villagers tested the prisoners, all young men, for bravery. All the women and children formed two lines, facing each other. Everyone held a stout stick or a thorny branch. One by one, the prisoners ran between the lines. The women and children struck at them with their sticks and branches. The men were soon bruised and bloody.

Two prisoners did not make it to the end. They staggered and fell. The village men killed them both, for they were not worthy.

The prisoners who did make it to the end of the line were worthy. They were adopted into the tribe. They were given to women whose

Mohawk war club

husbands or sons had died of sickness or been killed in war. They would take the places of those men. They would be warriors and hunters of the People of the Place of Flint.

One woman, whose husband had not come back with the rest of the war party, was not pleased. She did not want to let her newly adopted man live. And so, this man was put to death—but in a way that let him show his bravery. He was burned all over his body with torches and hurt in other ways until he was near death. Then he was killed, cooked, and eaten. In this way everyone gained a share of the man's courage.

When the war party that Bright Sky's father was in returned, it would be autumn. Then the men would stay in the village. They did most of their hunting and fishing in autumn, winter, and spring. Winter was also the time for making things that were needed—bows, arrows, paddles, snowshoes, bowls, and cups. The men carved these things out of wood. The women made clay pots, woven baskets, and clothing.

Bright Sky suddenly realized that his mother was speaking to him. Most of the women and children had finished eating. They were leaving the longhouse.

His mother and the other women were going to their patches of farmland outside the village. The farms, like the longhouses, belonged to the women. His mother had his baby sister strapped to her back in a cradleboard. When she reached her field, she would hang the cradleboard from a tree branch while she worked.

A year ago, Bright Sky would have gone with his mother. Then, he had had to help in the work with the corn, beans, and squash. But now he was eight summers old. It was time for him to learn the ways of a man. And the forest was the place of the man.

With some of his brothers, Bright Sky started toward the woods. Boys his age and older spent their days in the forest. There they learned the ways of the animals and how to hunt. They also played at war. When Bright Sky was a man, the forest would be his second home. Hunting and war would be the most important things in his life.

Mohawk ways

The Mohawk built their villages deep in the woods. They always selected a place close to a stream, so that they would have water for drinking and cooking. They cut and burned the trees around the village so that they could grow crops. Thus there was blue sky above a Mohawk village, and the sun shone down on the houses. But only a short distance away, on all sides, was the green, dark forest.

Each village was surrounded by a high wall of logs. The logs were stuck upright in the ground, side by side, and the tops sharpened to a point. The village farmland lay just outside the wall.

A Mohawk village might have four or five

The sap in sugar maple trees begins to flow in late winter or early spring. To get the sap, Mohawk women made cuts in the trunks of the trees. The sap dripped into bark buckets hung under the cuts. The women boiled the sap until it thickened into maple sugar.

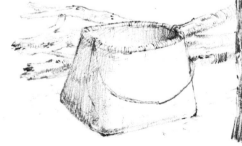

houses, or dozens. These houses, called longhouses, looked like long, narrow barns. The walls were made of thick sheets of elm bark, fastened to poles stuck in the ground. The roof was also made of elm bark. The men built the houses, but the houses belonged to the women.

As many as ten families—about fifty people—lived in a longhouse. Each family had a small, open "room." These rooms were on each side of the house. Cooking fires, shared by the two families across from each other, glowed in the fire pits at mealtime.

Both men and women wore long deerskin shirts and mocassins. These were often decorated with dyed porcupine quills. The men also wore a leather breechclout and leather leggings. The women wore a long skirt. In very cold weather, the women often put on short leggings that reached from just below the knee to the ankle.

If Mohawk men or women had to be outside for any length of time in very cold weather, they wore mittens and a cap made of beaver fur. And they might wrap themselves in a robe made of beaver fur. This robe was also used as a blanket at night.

In very hot weather, a Mohawk man usually wore only his breechclout and mocassins. A woman wore her shirt, skirt and mocassins. But on a very hot day she might wear only the skirt and mocassins.

Mohawk warriors usually wore their hair in a narrow ridge that ran from the forehead to the back of the neck. They plucked, shaved, or burned off the rest of their hair. Some men left only a scalp lock—a long lock of hair that

A Mohawk longhouse was smoky, drafty, noisy, and full of people and dogs. A row of fire pits ran down the middle. Narrow slits in the roof let out some smoke.

served as a challenge to their enemies. The women usually wore their hair in long braids.

If you had been a Mohawk child, your favorite dish might have been a soup made out of corn, beans—and a bear's head!

For food, the Mohawk depended on the animals of the forest and the crops grown on the farmland outside the village. Their main foods, which they called "the three sisters," were corn, beans, and squash.

Corn was used in a great many ways. Green corn was boiled, roasted, or made into soup. Ripe corn was dried and pounded into a coarse powder. This corn meal was baked into cakes or used to make a kind of mushy pudding. The Mohawk often boiled corn and beans together to make what we call succotash. This is a dish many people enjoy today. The Mohawk also ate another kind of corn that's popular now—popcorn. But they didn't put butter and salt on it.

Mohawk women cut pumpkins and other kinds of squashes into long strips. After drying the strips with heat, they stored them away for winter. They hung up ears of corn to dry, or stored them in bark containers for use in the winter.

Women and girls also searched in the forest for wild plant food. The Mohawk enjoyed mushrooms, berries, and nuts, which they ate raw or cooked. They also mixed them with other foods. And they ate boiled dandelions and other leafy plants.

The Mohawk usually roasted meat. Parts of animals that didn't have much meat on them—such as bear's head—were often skinned, cut up, and added to soup. Strips of deer meat and bear meat were dried and stored away for winter.

If you had been a Mohawk child, you might have eaten human flesh! The Mohawk sometimes killed, cooked, and ate prisoners. In this way, they hoped to make themselves as brave as the person they ate.

Mohawk comb made of carved bone

A Mohawk game you can play

The Mohawk and other Iroquois enjoyed a game they called "the dish." This game was played with six wild plum seeds ground down smooth and flat on each side. The Mohawk painted the seeds black on one side and white on the other.

To play the game, three or four people made a "pot" of one hundred dried beans. The plum seeds were placed in a wooden bowl. Each player took turns shaking the bowl and throwing the seeds into the air so that they turned over several times.

If the seeds came down so that three or four were black or white, the player passed the seeds and bowl to the next player. But if the seeds came down so that five or six were all one color, the player was a winner.

For five seeds of the same color, the player got to take two beans from the pot. If all six seeds were the same color, the player took twenty beans. The player also took another turn if he or she won any beans. When all the beans were gone from the pot, the player with the most beans won.

You can play this Mohawk game. Instead of wild plum seeds, use six buttons. Paint the buttons, or mark them, so that one side is different from the other. For the pot, use beans, as the Mohawks did, or anything you have on hand.

False-face medicine

The sick man lay in the longhouse. His wife sat cross-legged beside him.

Suddenly, from outside the longhouse, came the clatter of many rattles. There were grunts and weird cries outside the door. Then, a group of people in frightening masks came creeping in.

The sick man smiled feebly. The False Faces had come! Now, he would be well!

The Mohawk believed that certain kinds of sickness were caused by spirits, and could be cured only by spirits. So when Mohawk men and women got sick, they often sent for the False Faces to come and help them get well. The False Faces were men who belonged to a special club, or society. The masks they wore represented the faces of powerful spirits that could cure disease.

The society was made up of men who had once been sick themselves. While sick, they had dreamed of frightening faces. This meant the spirits were communicating with them. When the men were well, they became members of the society and a mask was made for them.

Each mask was carved on the trunk of a live tree, then removed. A mask carved in the morning was painted red. A mask carved in the afternoon was painted black. If the carving took both morning and afternoon, the mask was painted red and black. Strips of

These eighty-year-old Iroquois False-Face Society masks are like those made hundreds of years ago. But earlier masks had no metal parts or hair.

twisted bark were attached to the masks to look like hair. The masks were treated with great respect. They were often rubbed with oil and sprinkled with tobacco.

Wearing their masks, the False Faces went to the house of a sick person. They shook

their turtle-shell rattles over the sick one and sprinkled him or her with tobacco ashes. They sang in high, squawky voices, in a strange "made-up" language even they didn't understand. It was thought that this was how the spirits sounded.

After the False Faces visited a sick person, they were given gifts of tobacco and corn meal pudding. But these gifts were not for them. They were for the spirits that the carved masks represented.

While the False Faces wore their masks, they believed that the spirit of the mask was with them. They believed this gave them the power to cure sickness. The sick person believed this, too, very strongly. A visit by the False Faces often made a sick Mohawk feel much better, which might help him or her to get well.

A False-Face Society mask was carved from a live tree. Then the tree was cut down, the carving finished, and the mask painted.

Steam baths

The Mohawk, like nearly all the Indians of North America, enjoyed taking steam baths.

A Mohawk village was always near a stream or river. At the edge of the stream, the people built a small, dome-shaped hut for use as a bathhouse. This hut was made of a framework of branches covered with sheets of elm bark. It was just big enough for two or three people to sit in.

When the Mohawk wanted to take a steam bath, they built a large fire next to the hut. Then they dropped ten or twenty round stones into the fire. When the stones were red hot, the people used forked sticks to pull them into the bathhouse. Then the entrance to the hut was closed.

Inside the hut was a bark bucket filled with water. The Indians poured the water over the pile of red-hot stones. Clouds of steam filled the hut. The air grew thick and very hot. The people soon began to sweat. When they could no longer stand the heat and thick steam, they burst out of the bathhouse and plunged into the cool water of the stream.

For Mohawk and other Indians, the baths were a sort of religious ceremony. As they bathed, people prayed to the spirits they believed in. The Indians felt they made themselves pure by sweating. Warriors took a steam bath before going to war. Hunters often took a steam bath before a hunt.

Indians believed that steam baths kept them healthy. However, they probably also took these steam baths just because the hot steam made them feel good.

How the bow and arrow was invented

A Mohawk legend

One day, long ago, a young Mohawk brave named Ohgweluhndoe went into the forest to hunt bear. He carried a long spear with a point made of flint. This was the only kind of weapon the Mohawk had in those days.

Ohgweluhndoe traveled far through the woods. But he did not find any tracks or signs of bear. Then a thought came to him. Perhaps he would find a bear in the thick part of the forest in a place where he knew there were many grapes. It was autumn, the Moon of Falling Leaves. The grapes would be ripe and juicy. Surely, a bear would go there to eat the grapes.

The young warrior headed for the place of the grapes. When he reached it, sure enough, there was Oh-gwa-li, the bear, eating grapes. As he swallowed the grapes, he gave little squeals of pleasure, for Oh-gwa-li loves to eat grapes.

Ohgweluhndoe crept quietly up behind the big, black animal and raised his spear. But at that instant his foot slipped. He fell flat on his back.

The startled bear whirled around and charged toward the man. Ohgweluhndoe leaped to his feet and ran. Through the forest he went, dodging in and out among the trees, with Oh-gwa-li close behind.

Ohgweluhndoe knew he could not outrun the bear. Soon it would catch up to him and tear him to pieces! Then there would be no one to take care of his young wife and baby son. He would have to fight for his life! So Ohgweluhndoe stopped running and turned to face the bear.

He lifted his arm to hurl his spear at the charging animal. Once again, luck was against him! The end of the spear caught in a twisted grapevine that hung from a young ash tree. This slender sapling was a little taller than Ohgweluhndoe and about as thick as his wrist.

Ohgweluhndoe tried to pull the spear free. But the lower end of the vine was tangled in

a root at the foot of the sapling. All he did
was to bend the sapling backward in a curve.
Letting go of the spear, he turned and ran
for his life.

Before he had gone very far, he realized
that there was no sound behind him. He did
not hear the bear's heavy feet crunching on
the dry leaves. Looking back, he saw the bear
lying on the ground with the spear through
its neck! What had happened?

Ohgweluhndoe went back and looked down
at the dead bear. Somehow the spear had
come loose from the vine—with such force
that it had killed the bear.

The warrior pulled the spear from the
bear's neck. Once again he put the end of the

spear against the vine. Slowly, he pulled the spear back. The vine stretched, bending the sapling. Ohgweluhndoe let go of the spear. The sapling sprang upright. As the vine straightened with a snap, it hurled the spear through the air. Ohgweluhndoe had invented the bow and arrow.

The Mohawk soon learned how to make smaller bows out of small saplings. For the bowstring, they used animal hide instead of grapevine. And they learned to make small spears, or arrows, with feathers at the end to help them fly straight. The bow and arrow became their most important weapon.

From 1609 to today

The children looked at their teacher with interest. He had just told them he was an Indian—a Mohawk Indian!

He smiled at them. "Let me tell you something about my people. They played a big part in the history of the United States. Why, if it weren't for them, you might speak French instead of English!"

Tomahawks such as this one were made in Europe and traded to the Mohawk and other tribes for furs. This tomahawk is both an ax and a pipe.

"It was in 1609 when Mohawk warriors met the first white people they had ever seen. One of these men was the French explorer Samuel de Champlain. He was with a group of our enemies, Huron and Algonquin Indians. The French had guns—weapons we had never seen or heard of before. Champlain shot two of our chiefs, killing them.

"Because of this, the Mohawk and our Iroquois brothers became bitter enemies of the French. Many years later, when France and England were fighting to gain control of North America, we helped the British. People who study history think that if we had helped the French, the United States and Canada would have become part of France." He grinned. "That's why I said that but for us you might be speaking French!"

"Yes," he went on, "we Mohawk and the other tribes of the Iroquois League were a great and powerful people. Our League had laws that ruled all the tribes. Each tribe had a number of people called sachems (SAY chuhms). The sachems represented their tribe at meetings of the great council. There, new laws were made and problems were solved. It is even possible that some of the ideas for the government of the United States came from our League!

"At one time we controlled more than a thousand miles (1,600 kilometers) of territory—what is now about a dozen states of the United States. We conquered many tribes. We even believed that all the nations of the world might one day become part of our League.

"But during the American Revolution, when the colonies went to war to free themselves from British rule, our League split. Two of the tribes sided with the Americans. We Mohawk decided to help our old friends, the British. Our chief, Thayendanegea, whom white people called Joseph Brant, led Mohawk war parties against the Americans. He burned towns and killed many people. Americans grew to fear and hate him, but the English looked upon him as a true friend.

"To stop the attacks, American soldiers invaded our land. They burned our towns and killed our people. Most of us fled north, into Canada, which was British territory.

"A lot of Mohawk Indians still live in Canada. Many others are in New York State. Some of us live on reservations, but a great many live and work in Canadian and American towns and cities. We dress, talk, and live like other Canadians and Americans, but we are proud to be Mohawk.

Joseph Brant was a Mohawk chief at the time of the Revolutionary War.

The Nez Perce

People of the Western Mountains

The Nez Perce people lived in the high
country where the states of Idaho, Oregon,
and Washington come together. It is a land of
purple mountains, broad valleys, and great
forests of evergreen trees.

The Nez Perce lived in small groups of
thirty or forty people. During the summer,
each group traveled about a large area of
land that "belonged" to it. The men hunted
and fished. The women gathered wild plant
food. Wherever they stopped, the people built
little huts. In winter, each group stayed in a
small village of five or six underground
houses. These houses were round pits covered
by a cone-shaped roof.

Each group had a chief who was picked by
the group. This chief did not make laws or
give orders. He could only offer advice and
ideas. When there were problems to solve, or
decisions to be made, everyone in the group
had a vote.

Tribes living near the Nez Perce included
the Flathead, Coeur d'Alene, Cayuse,
Shoshone, Bannock, Klikitat, and Yakima. All
of these tribes lived in much the same way as
the Nez Perce.

The Guardian Spirit

The gray light of dawn began to push night's darkness from the sky. Slowly, the eastern horizon turned pink as the sun prepared to show its face. Then the red edge of the fiery ball appeared, rising behind the distant mountains.

The sun's brightness sparkled on the waters of a river that ran through a broad valley. Beside the river stood a village. It was a village of the people who called themselves *Nimipu*, meaning "We People."

As the sun rose higher, the man whose duty was to wake up the people made his way through the village. "I wonder if everyone is up?" he cried. "It is morning! We are alive, so thanks be! Rise up! Look about!" The village began to stir. Women started to prepare the morning meal.

A short time later, a boy left the village. He made his way toward a distant evergreen forest that marched up a steep hillside. The boy was about ten years old. He was beginning the most important event of his life. He was going in search of his Guardian Spirit.

This was something that every boy and girl did between the ages of nine and fifteen. It was a sacred, religious thing. For this reason, the boy was naked. He carried no weapons or food. He would not eat or drink or sleep until he met his Guardian Spirit.

The boy knew he faced a difficult and dangerous task. He would be alone, and far away from any help. He would be in danger from animals such as cougars and bears.

Many children became frightened, or hungry and thirsty. Some gave up before they met their Guardian Spirit. He hoped this would not happen to him. For, if he could meet his Guardian Spirit, he would have special power from then on!

He would also have a new name that the Spirit would give him. Now he had several nicknames that people had given him. But the name his Guardian Spirit would give him would become his real name.

Following a faint trail, the boy climbed through the forest until he came to a rocky ledge. The ledge was high up on a cliff that formed one side of the hill. From there, the boy could see the whole valley spread out for miles. He also seemed closer to the wide sky. It was a good place for his Spirit to come to him.

He gathered some rocks and piled them into a small mound. Then he sat down beside the mound, with his legs crossed, to wait. He tried to think only of his Spirit, calling to it silently within his mind.

The day wore on. The boy sat, hardly moving, staring toward the horizon. As the sun began to set, the forest behind him slowly filled with dark shadows. Soon, the creatures of night would be out hunting.

Darkness closed around the boy. He was frightened, but he was determined not to give up. All through the night he sat, trying to think only of his Guardian Spirit. When he grew drowsy, he pinched himself to stay awake. Lack of sleep, as well as hunger and thirst, would help him meet his Spirit.

When morning came, the boy was still

awake. He was very thirsty. His stomach rumbled with hunger. His eyelids closed and his head kept nodding. His thoughts were all mixed up. He couldn't tell what was real and what was not.

There was a long rumble of thunder that made him glance up with half-closed eyes. A dark shape sailed toward him out of the gray sky. It was an eagle! Swiftly, the eagle flew toward him. It was so close he could see its fierce eyes. Its sharp, curved beak opened. The boy heard the bird speak to him, in a voice like that of a human.

The boy's head jerked up. He realized that he had closed his eyes. The eagle was gone. The gray sky was empty. But the boy knew that he had seen his Guardian Spirit.

Proud, and wildly happy, he staggered to his feet and made his way back to the village. He told no one of his dream. He did not even tell his mother, Good Woman, nor his father,

No-Horns-on-His-Head. The dream was a sacred, secret thing that only he could know. But his parents and the others of the tribe could tell that he had been successful. When the time came, they would learn his name.

The boy ate some food and then went to sleep. The next day, his life went on as if nothing had happened. But he knew he now had the help and protection of his Guardian Spirit. It would aid him when he hunted. If he ever went to war against the southern people his tribe called "an enemy to be fought," his Guardian Spirit would be near.

Much of the boy's summer was spent away from the village. In early summer, the people went to a place where three rivers came together. Many tribes met there each year under a truce, or peace agreement, to trade with one another. Later in the summer, all the people of his village went up into the mountains. There they met people from other villages. The men and boys played games and gambled. The women dug the wild lily bulbs that grew on the mountainsides. These were an important food that would be stored for the winter.

Summer slipped into autumn and autumn gave way to winter. The people returned to the earth lodges in their permanent village for the cold months.

One winter morning, the man who woke the village called out: "People, lay all aside. Prepare yourselves. Tonight we will gather in the great dancing lodge for the Dance of the Guardian Spirit!"

This was the day the boy had waited for. He spent hours thinking of what was to

happen. That afternoon, he painted his body
with designs that would help him to look like
his Guardian Spirit, the eagle.

In the evening, all the people of the village
gathered for the dance. This was not a dance
for fun. It was a sacred dance—a religious
event. One after another, boys and girls who
had met their Guardian Spirit began to dance.
As they danced, they chanted the song of
their Spirit.

When the boy's turn came, he stepped into
the center of the circle. His words and
movements revealed to all that his Guardian
Spirit had blessed him with the name
Speaking Eagle.

A Nez Perce winter house was a deep, wide, round pit. A log was placed upright in the center of the pit. To form the roof, people laid poles, like the spokes of a wheel, from the top of the center post to the edge of the pit. They spread woven mats made of cedar bark, sagebrush, and other plants over the poles. Finally, they covered the mats with tightly packed grass and dirt.

Nez Perce ways

Speaking Eagle lived in two different houses. One was his winter house, the other, his summer house.

The winter house was a deep, round pit with a cone-shaped roof. Speaking Eagle and his mother and father shared the winter house with three other families. There were six such houses in this Nez Perce village.

In summer, the people often went away from the village for weeks on end. They moved around from place to place, seeking food. So, they had special summer houses they could put up and take down quickly.

A Nez Perce summer house was nothing more than a few poles covered with woven mats. It might look like a tepee, a slanted wall, or a circle of fence without a roof. Such a house simply gave shade and kept the wind from blowing out the cooking fire.

Because the Nez Perce did not grow any crops, they spent almost all their time searching for food. In early spring, when the snow began to melt and ground was soft and muddy, Nez Perce women searched for roots they called *kouse*. To dig up the roots, they used sharp digging sticks. The women boiled the roots to make a sort of pudding, or baked them into thin cakes.

Early in June, another important food had to be gathered. The Nez Perce called this "the time of the first run of the salmon." Then, the rivers of their land were filled with salmon swimming upstream to mate and lay eggs. For many days, the men and boys were able to catch huge numbers of fish.

Each spring, usually in early June, salmon filled the rivers in the Nez Perce country. Men and boys worked hard to catch as many as possible. Some splashed about in shallow water to spear or net the fish. Others fished from platforms of rock or wood built out from the shore. And some caught the fish in traps made of brushwood and poles.

All summer, women and girls searched for wild plant food. They collected wild onions, carrots, and lily bulbs, which were eaten raw or cooked. There were many kinds of berries. And in the autumn, there were nuts. Most of these foods could be dried or cooked, and then stored for use in the winter.

The men hunted deer, elk, mountain sheep, rabbits, and even bears and wolves with bow and arrow. But meat was always scarce, for animals were hard to catch in the open meadows and forested mountains.

Any fish that could not be eaten right away were stored for the winter. After cleaning the fish, the Nez Perce put some on wooden racks to dry in the sun. Others were smoked over a smoky fire.

The Nez Perce women used dried plant leaves to weave hats that looked like baskets.

In winter, the people had to make use of their stored foods. Bits of dried berry cakes were used to flavor dried fish, meat, and root cakes. This might be all they had to eat for weeks at a time. The stored food often ran out before spring came. Then, people might have nothing to eat but a mush made of roasted and ground up tree moss.

Speaking Eagle and other Nez Perce wore clothes made out of tree bark. The women made the clothes by weaving cedar bark together to make a kind of rough cloth.

In summer, men wore only a strip of bark cloth around the waist. Women wore small, bark-cloth aprons and foot coverings. They also wore caps that looked like baskets. They wove these out of dried plants. In cold weather, both men and women wrapped themselves in blankets made of rabbit skins.

How Coyote made people

A Nez Perce legend

Long ago, before there were any people in the world, all the animals lived together and could talk to one another. The cleverest of all the animals was It-su-yah-yuh, Coyote. He was their leader.

One day Coyote went away to visit friends in the east. While he was gone, the terrible monster Iltswetsix crawled out of the sea and came into what is now the land of the Nez Perce. Great and terrible was his hunger! When he opened his great cave of a mouth, he sucked in air with such force that animals were drawn into his stomach! He soon ate most of the animals in the land.

When Coyote came trotting back toward home, he heard the voice of Koh-koh, Crow, calling to him.

"It-su-yah-yuh!" called Crow. "The great monster Iltswetsix has sucked nearly all the other animals into his stomach! I only escaped because I was high in the sky!"

Coyote felt he had to try his strength and cunning against the monster. With Crow flapping after him, he hurried toward the valley where Iltswetsix lay.

When he came in sight of the monster, Coyote picked up a sharp rock. He used the rock to cut a number of tough vines. He tied himself to the earth with the vines and covered himself with grass. Then he called out to Iltswetsix: "Ha, you cannot see me!

Ha, I am part of the earth. You cannot swallow me as you swallow other things!"

In dreadful anger, Iltswetsix opened up his huge mouth and sucked in the air. The force was so great the grass shriveled and trees bent. The vines gave way, and Coyote was drawn into the monster's stomach!

This was really part of Coyote's plan. Inside the monster's stomach, he saw all the other animals. "Come," he urged them, "let us kill our enemy!"

But the others were all afraid. Even the great Bear and the poisonous Rattlesnake were afraid. Coyote was so angry he kicked Bear in the face. This is why Bear's face is flat. And Coyote stomped on Rattlesnake's head. This is why Rattlesnake's head is flat. Then Coyote took the sharp rock he had used to cut the vines and began to cut out Iltswetsix's heart.

The monster rolled and twisted in pain. Most of the animals were more terrified than

ever. But Fox came to help Coyote. Because of his bravery, Fox became nearly as smart and clever as Coyote.

Finally, Iltswetsix died. Then Coyote cut a hole in the monster's body so that all the animals could escape.

When they were all out, Coyote looked at the huge body. "What shall I do with this?" he wondered.

Fox thought for a moment. "Cut it up and make people out of all the different parts," he suggested.

So Coyote cut off the monster's head and made the Flathead people. He cut off the monster's feet and made the Blackfoot people. From each part of Iltswetsix, Coyote made a tribe of people.

At last, only the monster's heart was left. Coyote held it up and drops of blood fell from it onto the earth. From these drops of blood, people sprang up. They were taller, stronger, and braver than any of the other people Coyote had made. He was very pleased with them. Of course, they were the Nez Perce, the finest people of all!

So that is how all the tribes came into the world. As for the monster's heart, Coyote turned it into a great stone. He left it in the valley where he had defeated Iltswetsix. You can see the stone today, for it is still there!

"I will fight no more forever"

The evening sun tinted the Idaho mountains purple. On the Nez Perce reservation, an elderly woman and her grandson talked.

"Who was Chief Joseph?" asked the boy. "I've heard people say his name a lot."

"He was our greatest leader," his grandmother said. "He lived about a hundred years ago."

"Tell me about him" begged the boy.

She smiled. "Well, first you should know of things that happened before he was born. Then you'll understand him better.

"Before the white people came to America, we went about on foot. We hunted, fished, and gathered plant food. Then the Spanish brought horses to America. About three hundred years ago, we got horses from tribes to the south of us. The horses changed our way of life. We became skillful riders. We hunted buffalo from horseback. We began to live and dress like the Plains Indians.

"In the year 1805, a group of ragged, starving Americans came into our land. This was the Lewis and Clark Expedition. These men had been sent out by President Thomas Jefferson to find a way across the country to the Pacific Ocean. This was the first meeting between our people and the whites. We fed them, treated them as friends, and even sent some of our people with them as guides.

"After the Americans, French-Canadian fur traders came into our land. At that time we called ourselves *Nimipu*, which means 'We

People.' But the French saw some of us wearing bits of shell in our noses. So the French called us Nez Percé (nay perh SAY), which means 'pierced nose.' This is the name we have been known by ever since. Today, however, people say nehz PURS.

"But back to my story. Within a few years, missionaries, settlers, and then soldiers came. We did our best to stay friendly. But many of our people feared that the whites wanted our land.

"And the United States did ask our people and others to sign a treaty giving up some of our land to the white settlers. The government promised that the rest of the land would be ours forever. We were also promised money, schools, and other things.

"Although some of our chiefs feared it was a mistake, they signed the treaty. We hoped that by giving up some of our land we could keep the rest.

"But the government did not keep the promises. Then gold was discovered on the Nez Perce reservation by white men who had no right to be there. Before long, hundreds of gold hunters invaded our land.

"The government asked us to sign a new treaty, giving up even more land! This time, many Nez Perce chiefs refused. But some signed. So the government felt that all the Nez Perce people had to accept the treaty. The ones who refused to sign the treaty were known as Nontreaty Nez Perce. They stayed on their land. This was a cause of trouble. Many settlers felt that *they* owned the land.

"Finally, in 1877, the government called all the Nontreaty Nez Perce chiefs together.

They were told that they and their people must go to the reservation! The chiefs knew they had no choice. The American Army would force them to obey. They were angry and bitter. They felt the whites had stolen their land, lied to them, and cheated them.

"A number of Nez Perce went on the warpath. They killed some white settlers. Then American soldiers came to punish them.

Chief Joseph was a famous leader of the Nez Perce. He lived from 1840 to 1904. This photograph of him was taken about 1900.

This picture is from a painting called
The Surrender of Chief Joseph. *The artist,*
Frederic Remington, is famous for his
paintings of Indians and Western scenes.

That was when Chief Joseph became our war
leader.

"A missionary gave him the name Joseph.
His real name came from the Great Spirit in
a vision. It was Hin-mah-too-yah-lat-kekt, or
Thunder-rolling-in-the-mountains.

"And he did make the thunder roll. He won
many battles, even though he and his men
were badly outnumbered. But Joseph knew he
could never defeat the Army. So he led his
followers north, hoping to escape to freedom
in Canada.

"For almost four months, Joseph fought
and tricked and escaped the soldiers. He was
very near Canada when the soldiers finally
surrounded him. The Nez Perce battled for
five days. But in the end, they had to give up.
Many men were dead or wounded. The
women and children were freezing.

"When he surrendered, Joseph said, 'Hear
me, my chiefs. I am tired. My heart is sick
and sad. From where the sun now stands, I
will fight no more forever.' "

"What happened to Joseph?"

"He and his followers were sent to Kansas
and then to Oklahoma," his grandmother
said. "At last, after more than seven years,
some were brought back to this reservation in
Idaho. Joseph and some others were taken to
a reservation in Washington. The home he
loved—the Wallowa Valley of Oregon—he
saw only once again before he died.

"Today, there are about 2,400 Nez Perce.
Some of us live in towns and cities. But
most—about fifteen hundred—still live here
on the reservation—on land that has always
belonged to the *Nimipu!*"

The Hopi

Village Dwellers of the Southwest

The Hopi people lived in the southwestern part of the United States, in what is now Arizona. This is high desert country. Large, flat-topped, steep hills, called mesas, dot the broad land. Sagebrush, cactus, and other desert plants grow everywhere.

Several hundred years ago, about three thousand Hopi lived in villages on top of some mesas. They built stone houses covered with clay. These houses, all joined together, made a Hopi village look like a large, spread-out apartment house.

Very little rain falls in this country. When it does rain, the water runs down the sides of the mesas and soaks into the ground below. The Hopi had farms on the land below the mesas on which their villages stood. Most of their food came from their farms.

The Hopi did not have any chiefs. But certain men in each village acted as priests or leaders.

Living close to the Hopi, and much like them, were the Zuni and Keresan peoples. Nearby were the Havasupai and Walapai, but they were not farmers. The warlike Navajo and Apache also lived in this desert country.

Life in the desert

Bird-Ready-to-Fly sat on the ground beside her grandmother, Flute Maiden. They were making baskets of dried, twisted plant leaves. Flute Maiden's basket would be perfect, for she had made baskets for many years. She was an old, wise, and skillful person. But Bird-Ready-to-Fly was only eight. She was just learning how to weave a basket. She wasn't very good at it yet. Already, her basket looked lopsided!

The leaves for the baskets came from plants that grew in the desert. The desert was the home of Bird-Ready-to-Fly's people, the *Hopitu*, or "Peaceful Ones." It was a harsh, dry land, but the *Hopitu* knew how to get everything they needed from it.

Just the other day, Bird-Ready-to-Fly had watched some of the women build a new house. They built the walls with stones the men brought from the desert. Then they coated the stones with moist clay dug out of the desert. The clay dried smooth and hard in the warm sun.

Women also made pottery out of the clay. They made pots and jars to keep water in and to cook in. Bird-Ready-to-Fly often went with her mother, To-Dip-Water, to get clay for pots. They also brought back plants with which to make the colors and brushes used to decorate the pots.

The desert provided many plants used for all kinds of things. Some plants made a fine, slow-burning fuel for cooking, or for a warm fire on cold nights. The *Hopitu* used certain plants to make paints and dyes for coloring pots, baskets, or clothes. Some plants were cooked and eaten. Others were used to flavor foods. Bird-Ready-to-Fly had been taught what all these plants looked like. And she knew where to find them.

Indeed, everything the Peaceful Ones needed could be found in the desert. Of course, the one thing there wasn't much of in the desert was water. But the Peaceful Ones built their villages near springs, so as to have water for drinking and cooking. And they planted their crops below the mesas, where there was some water under the land.

The Peaceful Ones were farmers. Most of their food came from the land. Each clan, or group of related people, had its own land. The land belonged to the women of the clan. But the men did the farming.

Bird-Ready-to-Fly's father, Warming-by-the-Fire, spent much of his time in the fields. There was always a lot to do. In spring, he broke up the ground and planted the seed corn. He built little fences of dried grass. When the new plants began to peep up, the fences kept the wind from covering the plants with sand. Even so, some sand always blew through the fences. Then, he cleaned off the little plants very gently. And, of course, he pulled up weeds to give the little plants room to grow.

To grow tall and ripe, the corn and other crops needed rain. Rain was one of the most important things in the lives of the Peaceful Ones. Each year they held a very special ceremony to remind the spirits that rain was needed. Bird-Ready-to-Fly knew that it was the kachinas (kah CHEE nuhz) who sent rain.

The kachinas were great spirits who lived in mountains to the west. They looked after the weather.

Bird-Ready-to-Fly remembered last year's rain ceremony very well. The priests of the Snake and Antelope societies had done the snake dance. They did this dance every other year. They painted their bodies and wore special costumes. As the whole village watched, the priests danced and chanted.

The most important part came when the priests danced with live snakes held in their mouths or wrapped around their necks. At the end of the dance, the priests dropped the snakes onto a special design made of corn meal. Then they picked up the snakes and

turned them loose outside the village.
Everyone knew the snakes would hurry off to
tell the spirits of the need for rain.

Sometimes, certain men dressed up as
kachinas. In one ceremony, they went from
house to house, asking if the children had
been good for the past year. They threatened
to take the bad children away in the baskets
they carried with them.

When Warming-at-the-Fire wasn't working
on the farmland, he was always busy with
other things. He might make a pair of
moccasins or weave a blanket. The weaving
of cloth, from cotton grown on the farms,
was done only by men.

Sitting in the house in the evening,
Warming-at-the-Fire might work at making a
kachina doll or a prayer stick. The doll would
be used for religious ceremonies. But Bird-
Ready-to-Fly often played with the kachina
dolls her father made.

To make a prayer stick, Warming-at-the-
Fire used a slim twig of cottonwood. He
painted the stick and decorated it with
feathers held in place by cotton cord. After
breathing prayers onto the stick, he might
place it at the village spring, or on the
farmland, or up among the rafters of the
house. The feathers would carry his prayers
to the gods.

At times, Warming-by-the-Fire went to a
large underground room called a kiva (KEE
vuh). There were several kivas in the village.
Only men could go to a kiva. Bird-Ready-to-
Fly knew the men went there to talk
man-talk. She also knew that the kiva was a
place for special religious ceremonies.

Bird-Ready-to-Fly's mother, To-Dip-Water, was always busy, too. Now she was grinding dried corn into meal. Seeing Bird-Ready-to-Fly looking at her, she smiled. "Come, help me grind the corn," she said.

Bird-Ready-to-Fly put her half-finished basket aside and joined her mother. First, To-Dip-Water spread kernels of corn on a rough, flat stone. She used another flat stone to rub and press the kernels into a coarse powder. Then Bird-Ready-to-Fly ground the coarse powder on another stone, until the corn meal was fine and smooth. As they worked, mother and daughter sang a corn-grinding song together.

Hopi women made very beautiful bowls and jars from clay dug in the desert.

Hopi ways

The Hopi people ate corn as their main food. Hopi men grew the corn on little patches of farmland. Some of the corn was yellow, like most of the corn grown today. But the Hopi also grew red, black, purple, and even blue corn.

Hopi women heated the kernels to dry them out, then ground them into powder, or cornmeal. The women baked the cornmeal into thin sheets of bread. Or, they mixed it with water and cooked it in a pot. This made a mushy pudding without much taste.

Hopi men also grew beans and squash. The women collected many kinds of plants that grew wild in the desert. Some of these were eaten and some were used to add spicy flavors to food. The Hopi often put salt in their food. They got the salt from dried-up lakes in the desert. Sometimes they sweetened their mushy cornmeal pudding with the fruits of desert cactus plants.

Hopi men often spent much of their time in an underground room called a kiva. It was a sort of clubhouse for them. It was also used for religious ceremonies and special meetings. Women could not go into a kiva except on special occasions.

The Hopi kept flocks of tame turkeys and ate turkey meat once in a while. But they didn't eat much other meat. There just weren't enough animals in the desert to make it worth going hunting every day.

However, once in a great while, all the men of a village would go on a hunt together. If they were lucky, they might bring back some deer, antelope, or rabbits. Then the Hopi women would make a meat stew to go with the usual cornbread and vegetables. But this was really a great treat.

When a Hopi man got married, he went to live in his wife's house. Women owned all the houses in a Hopi village. They also did most of the work of building a house. Men only helped in the heavy part of the work. They carried rocks from the desert and put up the poles that held up the roof.

A Hopi house was just a single room. The walls were made of rocks piled on top of each other. The rocks were covered with plaster made of clay and water. Wooden poles were laid across the tops of the walls. Brush and dry grass were crammed between the poles and smeared with plaster to make the roof. The floor was also a thick coating of plaster.

The Hopi of today still live in such houses, in villages called pueblos. *Pueblo* (PWEHB loh) is a Spanish word meaning "village."

During the hot desert summers a Hopi man

Hopi men carved dolls that represented magical beings called kachinas.

Hopi women built the houses in which their families lived. They covered the stones with a plaster made of clay and water.

Young Hopi girls wore a hairdo that looked like the flower of the squash plant. Married women wore their hair in two braids.

wore only a sort of short skirt made of cotton. A woman wore a dress that was simply a square piece of cotton cloth. She wrapped the square around herself and fastened it over her right shoulder. Around her waist she wore a cloth belt. The Hopi men grew the cotton on the farms and wove it into cloth.

In winter there was sometimes snow on the mesas. Then, the Hopi wore moccasins of animal skin. The moccasins reached up to their ankles. Men would wrap themselves in cotton blankets. And both men and women wore robes made of rabbit fur.

Hopi men wove cotton into cloth for blankets and clothes. Hopi women never did any weaving.

A kachina mask

The Hopi believed in magical beings they called kachinas—powerful spirits that helped and protected humans. There were a great many kachinas. Each had a different face, clothes, and ornaments. At special times, Hopi men dressed up as kachinas. When a man put on a kachina mask, he felt that he actually took on the power of that kachina.

On the next page are instructions for making your own kachina mask.

Materials:

- brown-paper bag (large)
- brown-paper bag (small)
- cardboard (thin)
- construction paper
- crayon
- newspaper or tissue paper
- paintbrush
- poster paints
- scissors
- white glue

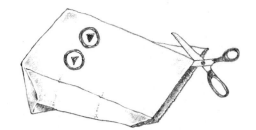

Push out the sides of the large paper bag. Cut the top corners, as shown, so the bag will fit over your shoulders. Put the paper bag over your head. Use the crayon to mark where the eyeholes should be. Take off the bag and cut out triangles or circles for the eyeholes. Then lay the bag flat, with the sides folded in and paint on the eyes.

Cut the corners at the open end of the small bag to make four flaps, as shown. Bend the flaps down and crease them. Stuff the bag with torn strips of newspaper, or with tissue paper. Coat the flaps with glue. Glue the flaps to the large bag to form the kachina's jaws. Paint teeth on the small bag.

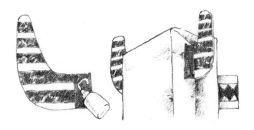

Cut two horn shapes out of the thin cardboard. Bend back a small part of the wide end of each horn to make a flap. Paint each horn. Coat the flaps with glue. Glue the flaps to the sides of the large bag to give the mask horns.

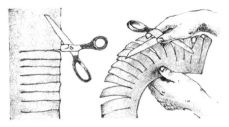

Cut two pieces of construction paper the same length as the bottom of the mask. Make a fringe of same-size strips along one edge of each piece, as shown. Curl the strips by running the edge of the scissors along each strip.

Glue the edges of the curled strips to the bottom of the mask. Make feathers out of construction paper, or use real feathers if you have them. Glue the feathers to the top of the mask. The pictures of kachinas on pages 98, 102, and 110 will give you ideas for decorating the mask and for making other kinds of kachina masks.

How people came into the world

A Hopi legend

When the world was new, there was darkness everywhere. There were no people or animals. At that time, there were really four worlds. There was the world we know now and three cave worlds beneath it, one under the other. Above these four worlds lived the Spirit Masters.

The first people and animals came into the lowest cave world. They quickly filled the cave to overflowing. They bumped and pushed each other in the darkness. There was hardly enough room to turn around! The cave was soon filled with dirt and disorder. The people began to complain in loud voices.

The Spirit Masters said, "This is not good. Someone must see what can be done to make things better." Two of the Spirit Masters, who were brothers, said, "We will make it better!"

The two brothers made a hole through the earth and through the roof of each cave. They then went down into the darkness of the lowest cave world. There, the brothers planted all the plants we have today. They hoped that one of the plants would grow tall and strong. The people and other animals could then use it as a ladder to climb up into the second cave world.

Most of the plants did not grow very tall. Others were not strong enough, or could not be climbed. But one plant did grow through the hole in the roof of the cave. This plant made a fine ladder. It was jointed and easy to climb. It was the cane plant. And ever since, the cane plant has grown in clusters along the Colorado River.

Many of the people and animals climbed up the cane plant into the second cave. This world was dark, too. The people could not tell how big the cave was. They feared it might be too small to hold all those who had been in the first cave. So they shook the ladder, knocking off those who were climbing up after them. Then they pulled the ladder up so that no one else could come up into the second cave world.

It wasn't long before the second cave was overcrowded, too. Then, some of the people and animals raised the cane ladder to the hole in the roof. They climbed up the ladder into the third cave world. Again, they pulled the ladder up so no one could follow.

The third cave was larger than the other two. But it was just as dark. So the two brothers found fire and showed the people how to make torches. In the light of the torches, the men set about building kivas.

But while the people lived in the third cave world, an evil came upon them. A strange sickness struck the women. They began to dance, hour after hour, stopping only to sleep. They did not cook meals for their families or take care of their children. They only danced and slept.

The men decided that the people and animals must leave the third cave world. Again the cane ladder was raised to the hole in the roof. The people and the animals

climbed up the ladder and through the hole, which is now called the Grand Canyon. They found themselves in the fourth world—the world in which we live.

This world, too, was dark, for at that time the sky covered the world like the roof of a cave. The world seemed damp and muddy. Even when the people lit torches, it was still too dark to see well.

The people, together with Spider, Coyote, Vulture, Swallow, and Locust, met to see how they might bring more light into the world. They decided that Spider should try first. So she spun a ball of pure white silk. It gave a little light, but not enough. The people put Spider's silk ball into the west, where it became the moon.

Then the people bleached a deerskin until it was pure white. They made it into a round shield that shone with brilliant light. They put the shield into the east. It became the sun. Now there was light in the world.

It so happened that while Coyote was in the cave world he had found a jar. He had brought this jar up into the fourth world with him. But the jar was heavy and he was tired of carrying it. He decided to leave it, but first he was curious to see what was in it.

Now that there was enough light to see by, he opened the jar. At once, a great many shining sparks flew out. The sparks scorched Coyote's face. This is why the coyote has a black face today. The shining sparks flew up into the sky and became the stars.

With all this light, the people could now see the world very well. Water surrounded the small bit of land.

The people and animals urged Vulture to spread his wings and fan the water to make it roll away. Then there would be more land. Vulture did so. As the water flowed away to east and west, great mountains appeared in the distance.

To help the people and animals, the two brothers cut deep grooves in the mountains to let the water flow through. As the water rushed through the grooves, it made them deeper and deeper. This is how the great valleys of the world were formed. The water has flowed away ever since. This is why there is more and more land and why the world becomes drier and drier.

People of Peace

"Why do we call ourselves 'Peaceful Ones'?" the young Hopi boy wanted to know. "Didn't we ever fight a war?"

The old man, who was a priest of the Pueblo, smiled. "We've always believed that war is stupid. But we did fight a sort of a war, once."

"Who did we fight?" the boy demanded.

The old man lit a stubby pipe. "We fought against the Spaniards. The Spanish explorer Francisco Coronado came here in the year 1540. He and his men wanted gold. They didn't find any, so they left. But Coronado claimed our land for Spain!

"After a while, a Spanish governor came with many soldiers and priests. He told us that we all belonged to the king of Spain! The Spaniards brought horses, sheep, and goats, as well as seeds for wheat and pepper plants. These things were useful to us. But the Spaniards also made harsh laws and treated us unfairly. If we didn't obey the laws, we were whipped or even hanged.

"The Spaniards also told us we had to give up our religion and accept their religion. Our religion has always meant a great deal to us. At one time, it was the most important thing in our lives. For some of us, it still is.

"We didn't want to give up our religion. And we hated the unfair laws. People of different Pueblos met in secret to plan an uprising against the Spanish.

"Our leader was named Popé (poh PAY). He was a medicine man of the Tewa people, from the Pueblo of San Juan, not far from Santa

Fe, New Mexico. News of when to strike was
sent by runners. The runners carried a piece
of knotted string that told us the day. On
August 11, 1680, the Pueblo people rose up
and attacked the Spaniards. We killed more
than four hundred of them. The others fled
into Mexico. Then we burned the churches
and houses the Spanish had built.

"We thought we were free again. But
fourteen years later, a Spanish army came.
They had many soldiers, with guns and

This wall painting shows the Hopi fighting against the Spanish in 1680.

cannons. We fought, but we didn't have a chance. The Spanish killed thousands of people from all the different tribes.

"We saw that we could never be truly free. But we worked out a different kind of freedom. We pretended to accept Spanish ways and their religion. But, secretly, we kept our own ways and our own religion. We had as little as possible to do with the foreigners living among us.

"Then, in 1800, Mexico fought a war to be free of Spanish rule. At that time, we were part of Mexico. The Mexicans won the war. Their government passed laws that freed us and the other tribes of the Southwest.

"In 1848, the United States fought a war against Mexico. The Americans took the desert country—our land—from Mexico. Our land became part of the state of Arizona. The United States agreed to let us keep our land and our way of life. For the most part, that promise has been kept.

"Before the Spanish came, there were many *Hopitu.* But the Spanish brought disease that killed us by the thousands. Today, there are only about six thousand of us. And here, in our Pueblo of Oraibi, there are only about three hundred of our people. But the *Hopitu* have lived in Oraibi for more than eight hundred years, so we will stay a little longer.

"Many of the older people still practice our ancient religion and follow the old *Hopitu* ways." The old priest smiled wistfully at the boy, who was wearing a T-shirt, jeans, and sneakers. "But a lot of the younger ones are becoming like other Americans."

The Tlingit

People of the Northwest Coast

The Tlingit people lived along the coast of what is now southern Alaska and northern British Columbia. This is not a cold place. The climate is mild all year.

Hundreds of years ago, many kinds of animals roamed the thick forests here. And immense numbers of fish and other creatures lived in the sea along the coast. It was easy for the Tlingit to get food.

This left them plenty of time to make things and to decorate things. Their large houses in the winter villages were often painted and carved with decorations. Many of the men were skilled woodcarvers. And many women wove beautiful blankets.

The Tlingit judged wealth by the number of furs, blankets, and other things a man owned. A wealthy man would sometimes give a great feast, now known as a potlatch (paht lach), at which he would give away much of his wealth. But he would get more back by going to the potlatches given by other wealthy men.

Just south of the Tlingit, lived the Haida and Tsimshian peoples. They were much like the Tlingit. To the north, lived a very different group of people—the Eskimo.

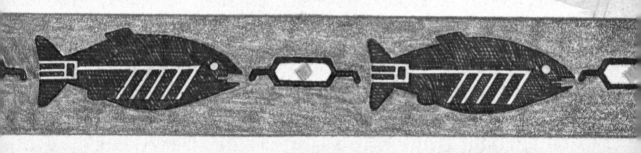

The great feast

The long, colorfully painted canoe, paddled by slaves, glided swiftly through the water. At the front of the canoe, a man in a bear costume danced about, tossing his head and waving his arms. At the back of the canoe, wrapped in fine blankets, sat a Tlingit chief, his wife, and their little boy.

The boy was excited. He and his parents were going to a great gift-giving feast to be held in honor of the raising of a chief's new emblem-pole. This did not happen often, for it was tremendously expensive to give a feast of this kind.

Years might be spent preparing for such a feast. All of the relatives of the chief giving the feast had to help. Large amounts of food had to be stored up, for the feast lasted for days. But most important of all were the gifts—blankets, carved boxes full of fish oil, furs, and other things.

Then, at the feast, the chief would give all the gifts away! He might even destroy some, just to show how rich he was. A really great chief might give away almost all he owned. This proved his wealth and power. The more he gave away, the more honor and respect he gained. And all of his relatives would share in his honor and respect, because they had helped him give the great feast.

The boy watched as the canoe headed toward a green strip of land in the distance. This was the island where the feast was to be held. Before long, the boy saw several tall, carved poles sticking up. Then the roofs of the houses came into view. The houses stood in a row on the beach. Behind the narrow beach, tall fir trees covered the land.

A number of canoes from other villages were also heading toward the beach. Of course, everyone invited to the feast had taken great care to be on time. To be late was to insult the chief giving the feast.

The boy's father ordered his slaves to paddle the canoe to a place behind the others. He was a young man and had been a chief for only two years. All the men in the other canoes were older, more powerful chiefs. It would not be proper for him to land before any of them. Such an insult might cause a war!

When the canoe finally landed, the boy's father, then his mother, and then the boy himself, stepped out, very slowly and solemnly. The slaves followed with the family belongings—bowls, spoons, baskets, finely carved boxes for holding fish oil, sleeping blankets, and other items.

A relative of the chief who was giving the feast greeted the boy's father. Presents were handed out at once. The family's bowls were filled with good things to eat. Slaves filled their beautifully carved boxes with fish oil in which to dip their food.

The boy's basket was filled with berry cakes. But he would find that this was only the beginning. He and his parents would receive many more things. And they would have so much food they wouldn't be able to eat it all.

Together, the family walked solemnly toward the feast-giver's house to meet him. The great chief and his wife stood beside the door. The chief was wrapped in a beautiful blanket decorated with emblems of his family. On his head he wore a special headdress of ermine tails. He greeted the young chief graciously. The boy's father was very respectful in return. The great chief's wife greeted them with a special smile, for the young chief was one of her relatives.

When he entered the house, the boy could hardly believe his eyes. Never had he seen so much food and wealth! Huge boxes of fish oil and piles of blankets and fur robes lined the wall. And the smell of smoked salmon, chunks of roasting deer and caribou meat, and baskets of berries and tasty roots made his mouth water. There was even a copper—

one of the big, flat pieces of decorated copper worth thousands of blankets!

For the rest of the day, the boy and his parents spent their time meeting the other guests, listening to singers, watching the dancers and actors—and eating. The merriment went on long into the night, with everyone grouped around the blazing fire in the great chief's house. Once, the boy almost shouted with delight when the chief had a slave throw a whole box of costly fish oil onto the fire! The flames shot up almost to the roof. How wealthy the chief must be to burn up so much fish oil!

On the third day, the real business of the feast took place. The guests sat on mats of

woven cedar bark outside the great chief's
house. The wealthiest and most powerful
chiefs sat closest to the chief giving the feast.
Less important chiefs sat farther away. Each
man knew exactly where he belonged.

When all was ready, the Speaker stepped
forward. He was a specially chosen man, a
chief himself, as great as the chief giving the
feast. He carried a carved wooden staff, the
"talking stick," that showed he was the
Speaker. Holding up his staff, the Speaker
shouted, "The time has come to raise the
emblem-pole."

Until that moment, the pole had been
hidden. Now, a crew of men dragged it to the

hole in which it would stand. By means of ropes, the men pulled the tall, heavy pole upright, so that it stood in front of the chief's house. A large hole at the bottom of the pole was now the entrance to the house. Above the opening, large figures had been carved on the pole. Each figure was painted in bright colors.

The boy listened carefully as the Speaker told the stories of all the figures, and why each was important to the chief. The stories took a long time, but the boy enjoyed them. They explained why the chief was so important. Many of the great people in the chief's family had been helped by spirit animals. The figures on the pole stood for some of the people and animals.

The stories over, dancers came leaping and shouting to entertain the guests. They wore masks and special costumes. Their dances acted out the stories the Speaker had told.

Much more happened during the day. Children of the chief's family-group who had reached a certain age were introduced to the guests. Then there was more dancing—and more eating! Finally, the time came for the great gift-giving.

The chief started with the most important guest. He gave this man blankets, fur robes, and other valuable things. The boy knew by the way the man accepted the gifts that he was pleased. If the man had thought the presents were not good enough, he would have dragged the blankets on the ground as

he walked away. This would have been a dreadful insult to the chief!

Each of the other guests, in order of importance, received similar presents. The boy was excited, for he could see that the chief had given away almost everything!

The chief then picked up the copper that was worth a fortune in blankets. To show that he had so much wealth it didn't matter, he cut off a large piece from the copper and threw it into the fire, where it melted!

Truly, the great gift-giving feast had been wonderful. The chief had shown he was an important and wealthy man. But the boy knew that the chief would get back all—and perhaps more than—he had given away. For every man who had been a guest would now have to hold a gift-giving feast.

The chief would be invited to each feast. He would receive many fine gifts. The men holding the feasts would try to give the chief more presents than he had given them. Even though the chief had given away most of his wealth, he would get back much more!

When the time came to leave, the boy eagerly climbed into his father's canoe. He was anxious to get home so that he could play at having a gift-giving feast. He and the other children would use sea shells, stones, and bits of wood for the gifts.

The boy knew that when he was older he would go to live with his mother's family. They would help him gain wealth. One day he would have many blankets and robes. Then he would hold a real gift-giving feast. He would show what a great and important person he was!

Tlingit ways

A Tlingit never went hungry. There was plenty of food for all the people who lived along the northwest coast. From the ocean, they got many kinds of fish and sea animals such as seals, porpoises, and sea otters. Along the shore, plenty of clams could always be found. In the nearby mountains and forests, men hunted deer, elk, and mountain goats. Women gathered berries, wild plant roots, and seaweed.

One of the most important Tlingit foods was fish oil. This came from a small fish called a candlefish, or *oolakan*. The fish was boiled until the oil came out. The oil was skimmed off the water and stored in wooden boxes. The Tlingit dipped almost everything they ate into this oil. It was like a sauce for them.

The Tlingit ate one meal at about ten o'clock in the morning and another at sunset. People usually ate in their houses. They sat on the wooden floor. The food was placed on a mat made of woven cedar bark. Before eating, people rinsed their mouth with water. This was good manners—and good manners were very important to the Tlingit, especially when they ate.

A slave, who was a person captured in a raid on another tribe, handed out bunches of soft, shredded cedar bark. People wiped their hands on these "napkins." Then they washed their hands in a bucket of water the slave gave them. They dried their hands on the shredded bark.

Each person then took a drink of water

This Tlingit spoon was made from the horn of a mountain sheep.

from a special drinking bucket. Everyone took a long drink. They wouldn't drink again until the meal was over. To drink during dinner was very bad manners!

A meal might begin with dried fish and bowls of fish oil. People dipped the fish into the oil before each bite. Of course, their fingers got very greasy. When they were finished, a slave again handed them a "napkin" and bucket of washing water.

Next came the cooked food. This was served in wooden dishes. People ate this part of the meal with spoons carved from the horns of mountain goats. Everyone was careful to take only small sips, and never open their mouth wide enough to show their teeth. That would be very impolite. After finishing the cooked food, the people again washed their hands.

The final course might be a big bowl of dried berries mixed with fish oil. When the meal was over, everyone again washed their hands. And now they could all take a long drink of water.

In summer, most Tlingit men usually worked in or near the sea. Because the weather was warm and they were often soaking wet, they wore only a deerskin breechclout. Women usually wore only a deerskin skirt.

In winter, women often wore two skirts, one over the other. In cold or rainy weather, men and women wrapped themselves in blankets woven from cedar bark and the wool of mountain goats. They might also wear woven hats made of cedar bark. These looked like upside-down baskets. But even on the

Every Tlingit family had one or more chests in which to store things. These cedarwood chests were beautifully carved and painted.

At the back of a Tlingit house were sleeping compartments for the chief and other important people. The compartments were often small copies of the main house. The chief's compartment was usually painted with designs.

coldest days, both men and women usually went barefoot.

The Tlingit and their neighbors were the only Indians who built their houses out of wooden boards. A Tlingit village looked much like a number of big barns clustered together. The first Americans to come to the Northwest were surprised to see these large wooden buildings, made with stone tools and put together without nails.

Tlingit houses were made of cedarwood.

But cedar trees were rather scarce. Men had
to search the forests for them. Then they had
to be cut down and trimmed—with only stone
tools for the job—and brought back. The man
who wanted a house often had to trade with
other villages to get all the logs he needed. It
took a lot of time and many people to build a
Tlingit house. Only a wealthy and important
man, such as a chief, could afford it.

The house was started by building a frame

This Tlingit blanket was made from mountain goat wool and cedar bark.

Women wove the blankets that Tlingit people wore. As they worked, the women followed patterns painted on boards that they kept beside them.

of stout logs and planks. Then the sides and roof were covered with boards. To make the boards, men pounded wedges into the ends of cedar logs. This caused long flat pieces to split off. The Tlingit knew how to split logs into boards almost exactly the same size.

When a house was finished it might be as much as forty feet (12 meters) long and thirty feet (9 m) wide. Several families lived in each house. The house had no windows. The doorway was a large round or oval hole.

The floor of the house was made of boards. There was usually a built-in bench running all around the inside walls. In the middle of the floor was a large pit, used as an open fireplace. All the women of the house shared the fire to cook for their families. Boards in the roof above the fireplace could be slid aside to make an opening to let smoke out.

A Tlingit village usually had only a few of these big houses, built close together in a row. The villages were by the sea. The doorways of the houses always faced the water.

Raven

Eagle

Hawk

Beaver

Thunderbird

Totem poles

In the villages of the Tlingit—and most other Northwest Coast people—there were usually many tall poles. Carved on the poles were great grinning and frowning figures, one above the other.

These poles are now called "totem poles." A totem (TOH tuhm) is a symbol, usually an animal, that stands for a tribe, clan, family, or person. A totem pole was a sort of "signboard" that told about a person's family. Totem poles served as entrances to houses, to honor the dead, and to mark graves. Only a chief or a very wealthy person could afford to have a tall totem pole as the doorway to his house. Such a pole told everyone that he and his family were noble, great, and important.

Some of the figures on a totem pole stand for ancestors. These are often shown as animals, because every chief believed that a magic animal had started his family. He also believed that magic animals had often helped or even married some of his ancestors. All this was told in the legend of the chief's family. The chief picked out the parts of the legend he wanted to show on the pole.

The artists who carved totem poles were greatly respected and well paid. They always carved the magic animals the same way on every pole. Raven always had a straight beak. Eagle had a curved beak. Hawk had a beak that curved nearly all the way back. Beaver had two big front teeth. The mythical Thunderbird—who made thunder by flapping its wings and lightning by blinking its eyes— had outstretched wings.

These Tlingit totem poles were carved long ago. They now stand in a park in Saxman, Alaska. The bird at the top of each pole is the Raven Spirit, Yethl.

Where mosquitoes came from

A Tlingit legend

Long ago, there lived a terrible giant known as Goo-teekhl. Fierce and cruel, he hunted men so that he could eat their hearts and drink their blood! For many years he had raided the villages of the Tlingit.

Many brave men tried to kill Goo-teekhl, but with no success. When they shot arrows into his chest he did not die. Perhaps, they thought, his heart is not in his chest. So they shot arrows into his arms and legs, hoping to hit his heart. But it was no use. They could not kill him. They knew then that there was no way to kill Goo-teekhl unless someone could find out exactly where his heart was.

One day, a brave man thought of a plan to find out where the giant's heart was. The man lay down on his blanket and pretended to be dead. Before long, Goo-teekhl came by. Seeing what he thought was a dead man, the giant touched the body. It was still warm, as if the man had not been dead long.

The giant grinned in delight. "I will eat his heart and drink his blood," he exclaimed. He then picked up the man. The man let his arms and legs dangle and his head hang down, as if he were truly dead.

Goo-teekhl carried the man to his house and put him down on the floor. Then the giant went out to look for his slave. The moment the giant disappeared, the man leaped to his feet. He seized a bow and arrow lying nearby.

Just then, the giant's slave came into the house. The man drew back the bowstring and aimed the arrow at the slave. "Tell me where your master's heart is," he said, "or I will kill you!"

"Do not kill me," pleaded the slave. "My master's heart is in his left heel."

Moments later, the man heard Goo-teekhl returning. As the giant came into the house, the man shot the arrow into his heel. With a dreadful cry, the giant fell to the floor.

As Goo-teekhl lay dying, he looked up at the man who had shot him. "Even though you burn my body to ashes, I will still drink your blood," he boasted. Then he died.

This angered the man. To prove that the giant's boast was false, the man dragged the giant outside and burned his body. When only ashes were left, the man scooped these up and threw them into the air. The wind scattered them far and wide.

But, alas, it had been a trick! Goo-teekhl had fooled the man. Each bit of ash became a mosquito—the first mosquitoes in the world. And, just as the giant had boasted, mosquitoes still drink people's blood!

This picture was taken at a Tlingit gift-giving feast, or potlach, that was held about eighty years ago.

Furs, gold— and poverty

The captain of the fishing boat wore a red checkered shirt and blue jeans. He looked like all the men who made a living fishing off the coast of Alaska. But there was one difference. The captain was a Tlingit.

He stared at the distant, snow-tipped mountains. "Things are better now for some of us," he said. "But many of us are still poor." He shook his head sadly. "Long ago, we had plenty. That was before the Russians came here in a ship in 1741. They were the first white people we met. It wasn't a friendly meeting. Some Russians came ashore in boats, to get fresh water. Our people killed them and took the boats!

"When the men didn't come back, the ship sailed away. But the Russians claimed the land. They named it Alaska, from an Indian word that means 'great land.'

"In 1799 the Russians came back. They built a fort where the city of Sitka is now. In 1802, the Tlingit attacked the fort and killed the settlers. Two years later, the Russians attacked us. They beat us, badly. After that, they ruled us harshly for many years.

"In 1867, the American secretary of state, William Seward, made a deal with the Russians. The United States bought Alaska. For a long time, we were left alone. Our way of life was almost as before.

"But then, in 1896, gold was discovered not far from here, in a place called the Yukon. Thousands of people came, hoping to become rich. Suddenly, everything changed. Many gold hunters took our land. Soon, all we had left were our villages."

The captain sighed. "We didn't have any great chiefs or leaders. We never fought against the Americans. And we were never given a reservation. We were terribly poor and miserable. To survive, Tlingit men took jobs in factories where fish is put into cans."

"For years, the Alaskan tribes asked the United States government to pay for the land that was taken from us. Finally, in 1971, the government gave the Alaskan Indians forty million acres of land and millions of dollars as payment. We Tlingit and some other tribes have banded together and started businesses.

"So, as I said, things are getting better for some of us. But we were poor for a long, long time. And many of us are still poor.

"But, in the last few years, we've rebuilt a few of the old houses to use for special events. And some of our young men and women perform a few of our old dances."

The Osage

Village Dwellers of the Plains

More than three hundred years ago, about six thousand Osage lived on the southeastern edge of the Great Plains. This area takes in parts of what are now Missouri, Illinois, Arkansas, and Oklahoma.

The Osage believed they came from the stars. They named the sky, the earth, the waters, and all the animals. To themselves, they gave the name *Ni-U-Ko'n-Ska*, meaning "Children of the Middle Waters." The name *Osage* they got from Europeans. It comes from *Wazhazhe*, the name of one of the three bands that made up the tribe.

The Osage lived in villages near the edge of the Plains. Two or three times each year, the Osage left their villages to go on a great buffalo hunt. The buffalo was their main source of food and clothing.

Each Osage village had two chiefs. One led the warriors in time of war. The other chief led all the people in time of peace. A group of wise men, known as "The Little Old Men," made all the laws.

Tribes living near the Osage included the Kiowa, Caddo, Kansa, Missouri, Pawnee, Illinois, and Quapaw.

The buffalo hunt

Eats Grass squatted near the edge of the camp, listening for the distant thunder of hoofs. Very soon, he knew, the men would force the buffalo herd toward the cliff. Then he and everyone else would have plenty of work to do.

It was early summer, and hot on the plain. Eats Grass wore only a breechclout and mocassins. His head was shaved, so that only a fringe of hair ran around it. He could not wear the long hair-strip of a man. Eats Grass was only eight summers old—not even a person, yet. But he would become a person in two more years. Then, he would be given his name. "Eats Grass" was just a nickname his playmates had given him.

Nearly everyone from the village was on the buffalo hunt. Only a few old people, and women with very small children, had stayed behind. They would look after the crops that had just been planted.

The men, women, and children—and dogs pulling wooden frames loaded with supplies—had marched across the plain for several days. Along the way, they camped at places the tribe had used for generations. The two chiefs—the Sky People chief and the Earth People chief—had gone ahead to pick out the hunting camp.

Eats Grass knew that the two chiefs took great care in choosing the place for the camp. It had to be near the cliff over which hunters would drive the buffalo. And it had to be a place they could defend. There was always a chance that while everyone in camp was busy after the hunt, their enemies, the *Pa-I'm*, or Long-Haired People (the Pawnee) might attack them!

Eats Grass found it exciting to come on this hunt with his father and mother. There had been work to do along the way, of course. Tender young plants were springing up on the plain, and many kinds were good eating. The people stopped often so the women and children could gather plants.

But there had been time for play, too, especially in the evening at the camping places. Eats Grass and the other boys played buffalo hunt, with some of the dogs as buffaloes. And at one camping place there was a stream with high, muddy banks. The boys played otter—sliding down the bank on their stomachs, into the water.

Suddenly, Eats Grass heard the great rumbling sound he had been listening for. And he heard loud shouts. The buffalo drive had begun!

He could imagine what was happening. His father, Reaches-the-Sky, had told him what went on. First, certain men went toward the herd. They kept the wind behind them, so the animals would smell them. This made the buffalo nervous. They began to move away from the smell. The men had picked a time when the herd was between them and the edge of a nearby cliff. To get away from the man-smell, the buffalo had to move toward the cliff.

Other men lay hidden behind piles of stone and brush on each side of the herd. As the buffalo began to move, these men jumped up, shouting and waving fur robes. The startled buffalo began to move faster to get away from the jumping, waving figures.

The buffalo were in a trap! The row of men on each side formed a big V. The buffalo were inside it. And the point of the V was the edge of the cliff. The terrified buffalo had no choice. If they tried to go to one side or the other, the men quickly set fire to piles of brush. Frightened by the flames and smoke, the buffalo pressed close together. Staying between the rows of men, the herd stampeded toward the cliff.

When the animals at the front of the herd came to the edge of the cliff, they tried to stop. But it wasn't possible. The rushing animals behind them pushed them over the edge. Before the herd could stop, many buffalo had fallen off the cliff—breaking their legs and injuring themselves so they couldn't move.

Other men, who had been waiting at the base of the cliff, went to work. They killed the injured animals with spears and clubs.

Osage buffalo-stomach bag

Soon, great, shaggy bodies lay everywhere.

Then the work of skinning and butchering began. Every part of a buffalo was used for something. The skins were made into robes and clothing. Hooves were boiled down and made into glue. Horns were carved into spoons. The long, stringy tendons that connected muscles to bone were made into bowstrings. Hearts and stomachs were dried and used as bags. Fat was used for making paint. Bones became tools.

Most important, of course, was the rich, red meat. Men cut the meat off in strips. Eats Grass, with all the other children, the women, and old men, began to carry loads of meat back to the camp. There, the women smoked the meat slowly over smoky fires, to preserve it. The whole village would live off the smoked meat for several months.

The hunt had been a great success. Everyone was excited and happy. It was much like a holiday! While the women smoked the meat, long lines of children continued to bring in more. Nearby, the men cooked the ribs of slain buffalo. That night, they would have a great feast.

Everyone had helped in the hunt, so the dead buffaloes belonged to all. The meat, skins, horns, tendons, and other useful parts were divided up among the "fireplaces," or family groups, of the tribe. There were twenty-two of these groups, with many people in each. The members of each "fireplace" would share the meat and other things among themselves.

These people, who called themselves the Children of the Middle Waters (and are now

Osage women made bags out of buffalo stomachs. To shape a bag, they put the stomach into a hole and filled it with melted fat.

called the Osage) returned to their village in late July. They stayed there while the women harvested the crops on their little patches of farmland. Then, in September, they set out again on another buffalo hunt. This hunt would provide them with a supply of meat for the winter.

Although the Osage hunted all kinds of animals, and raised corn and other crops, the buffalo was their main source of food and materials. The buffalo was very important to them. They thought of the buffalo as a sacred creature. They believed that when they came from the sky, it was the buffalo that gave them corn and squash and all the other things they needed.

farmland

main street

chiefs' houses

men's
bathing
place

women's
bathing
place

water lily
gathering
place

Osage ways

An Osage house looked like a wide, long hall with a low, curved ceiling. The walls were made of two rows of poles stuck upright in the ground. The tops were bent in and tied together. Other poles were tied crosswise. The Osage covered this framework with mats made of dried plant leaves woven together. The mats overlapped so that wind and rain couldn't get in.

A row of stout posts down the middle of the house held up the roof. A row of fireplaces ran alongside these posts. The fireplaces were just shallow pits dug in the earth floor. The women who lived in the house did all their cooking in these fire pits. An opening in the roof above each pit let smoke out.

Most of the floor was covered with woven mats like the ones on the walls and roof. During the day, the Osage sat on the mats. At night, they slept on them.

Hanging from the walls and ceiling were skin bags of dried meat, ears of dried corn, braided lily roots, and strips of dried pumpkin. These were for wintertime meals. They had to be kept up high so the village dogs couldn't steal them.

The Osage cut up water lily roots and dried them. They hung the dried roots in their houses to use for food during the winter.

The Osage were divided into two groups—Sky People and Earth People. The Sky People lived on the north side of the main street and the Earth People on the south side. All doorways faced east. The chief of the Sky People and the chief of the Earth People lived across from each other, in large houses. The chiefs usually had equal power. But the Sky chief led in time of peace and the Earth chief in time of war.

Osage warriors shaved off all their hair except for a narrow strip called a roach. They often tied animal hair and other decorations, such as the one in the photograph above, into the roach.

Women and girls wore their hair in braids. They painted the part in their hair red.

Some Osage women had a spider, a symbol of the spirit of life, tattooed on the back of their hand.

Summers are long and hot in the prairie country where the Osage lived. Men usually wore only a deerskin breechclout and moccasins. Women wore a long skirt and a short cape around their shoulders. In very hot weather, they might wear only a skirt.

In cool weather, or when they had to walk through thick underbrush, men wore leggings. The Osage often rubbed the leggings with gypsum—a white, powdery mineral. This made the leggings grayish white. The leggings had fringe that looked

Women and children gathered water lilies for food. The seeds and roots were eaten.

like the feathers on the legs of a golden eagle. The Osage had a special liking for the golden eagle.

In cold weather, Osage men and women wrapped themselves in long robes of buffalo skin. The furry part was worn on the outside. The inside was often painted with designs and decorated with colored porcupine quills. The women made and decorated the clothes.

Osage women did all the farming on little patches of land near their village. In late summer, the women picked the corn. Some of it was boiled and eaten right away. But a lot of ears were hung up to dry. Women ground the dried kernels into powder. The men often took plain corn powder with them to eat while away hunting. It was so light they could carry a lot of it. It didn't taste very good, but it filled their stomachs. The powder was also mixed with water to make a kind of cereal.

The women also grew squashes and pumpkins. When these were ripe, the women peeled them and took out the seeds. Then they cut the yellow and orange insides into strips and hung the strips in the sun to dry. When the strips dried, the women braided them together and hung them in the houses for winter food.

Women and children gathered many wild plants for food. A favorite was water lilies. The roots were boiled and the seeds were eaten raw or roasted. Persimmons (a wild fruit) were squashed into lumpy cakes. These cakes were baked over a fire, on a flat wooden "frying pan." The Osage put their food in wooden bowls. They ate with spoons made from buffalo horns.

Quill designs

The Osage, and other tribes, used porcupine quills for decoration. They pressed the quills flat, dyed them different colors, and wove them through things. You can make quill designs with plastic straws.

Materials:
- cardboard box top
- transparent tape
- magic markers or crayons
- scissors
- straws

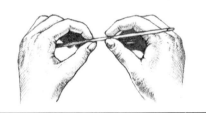

Flatten each straw by running your fingernail along it, *hard*, several times. Color the flat straws with magic markers or crayons.

With the scissors, make rows of slits in the box top, as shown. You may have to punch the holes with a sharp pencil first. Each slit should be a little wider than a flat straw. Leave a small space between slits.

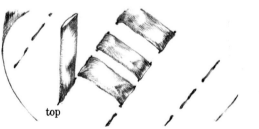

top

Push a straw through an end slit, so only a small part sticks out on the underside of the box top. Fold this piece over and tape it to the underside. Push the rest of the straw through the end slit in the opposite row. Lace the straw through the other slits, back and forth from row to row.

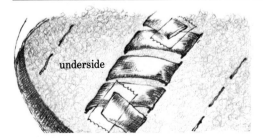

underside

When only a short bit of the straw is left, tape it to the underside of the box top, as shown. Lace straws through the slits in the other rows in the same way.

The choice of the Earth People

An Osage Legend

The Osage people, the Children of the Middle Waters, came from the stars. When they were new upon the earth, they were divided into three groups: the People of the Sky, the People of the Waters, and the People of the Land. On earth, they found a fourth group, the Earth People.

The wise men, called the Little Old Men, divided all the people into "fireplaces," or family groups. It was decided that each group needed a symbol. So the Little Old Men sent each group out to search for an animal, plant, or other thing that might be its symbol.

Of course, it would be a great honor for any of the "little people," the birds, animals, stars, plants, or insects, to become the symbol of a group. The leader of each group knew that many creatures would ask for the honor. Great care had to be taken to choose a truly fitting symbol. If the symbol chosen turned out to be a poor one, the group and all of its descendants would have trouble forevermore!

The group known as the Earth People traveled many days in their search. They crossed the plains and prairies, climbed hills, and walked through valleys. Many creatures came to their leader and asked to be made the group's symbol. But the leader did not pick any of them.

One day, the Earth People came across the trail of a deer. The leader pulled out an arrow and notched it to his bowstring. Slowly and carefully, he followed the trail. After a time, he saw a white-tailed deer ahead, among the trees. Raising his bow, he moved forward.

But suddenly his nose tickled and there was a haze before his eyes. He had walked into a large spider web! The sticky silk clung to his face. As he raised his hand to brush the web away, the deer saw the movement. In an instant, it had dashed out of sight.

Many of the people in the group laughed at what had happened. But the leader was not amused. Because of the spider web, he and his people would have no deer meat this night. Picking the sticky silk from his face, he looked angrily at the spider, which had crawled to the top of its torn web.

"You bad little black thing!" the man exclaimed. He struck at the spider with the end of his bow.

The spider dodged aside. The man lifted the bow again, but the spider put up its legs to protect itself.

"Where are you going that you do not look where you walk?" the spider cried.

The man lowered his bow. "I am the leader of the Earth People of the Children of the Middle Waters," he said proudly. "We are in search of a symbol."

"Then your search is ended," said the spider. "I shall be your symbol."

The people put their hands over their mouths to hide their smiles. Trying hard not to laugh, the leader asked, "Ah—do you have the courage and cunning of the panther?"

"No, I do not," said the little spider.

"Perhaps then you have the strength of the bear?" said the man.

"No, I have not," said the little spider.

"Well, then, do you have the dignity and grace of the wapiti?" questioned the man.

"No," said the little spider. "But all things come to where I build my house. And there they are destroyed."

The leader thought about this. He realized that the spider was crafty, for it set a trap for its prey. And it was patient, for it waited for its food to come to it. If the Earth People of the Children of the Middle Waters had the craftiness and patience of the spider, they would be successful in hunting and war.

So they chose the spider as their symbol.

Mohongo was an Osage woman who traveled to many parts of the United States and Europe. This painting of Mohongo and her son was done in 1830.

The land of my fathers

The rancher patted the neck of his beautiful horse. "I really love horses," he said. "Maybe it's because horses meant so much to my ancestors."

"What do you mean?" asked his friend.

"Well, you know I'm three-quarters Osage," said the rancher, "and horses were mighty important to the Osage. For hundreds of years, they did all their traveling and hunting on foot. But about three hundred years ago, they got horses.

"An Osage legend tells that they got the horses from the Kiowa people, who lived farther south. After they got horses, the

Osage soon became good riders. From then on, they hunted the buffalo on horseback.

"At about the time they got horses, the Osage also met the first European people they had ever seen. Two French explorers came to an Osage village. To the Osage, the men seemed pale and very hairy. The Osage called these men *I'n-Shta-Heh*, or 'Heavy Eyebrows.' This became the Osage name for all white people.

"Later, more Frenchmen came to the prairie lands. They claimed it for France. They named it Louisiana, after the French King Louis. Most of the French were traders. They gave the Osage metal axes, pots, and other things for furs. The Osage became very friendly with the French. When France was at war with Great Britain in the 1750's, Osage warriors helped the French.

"France lost the war, and Great Britain took over a large part of North America. This didn't matter to the Osage. They lived far to the west of the British colonies. And it didn't matter after the colonies revolted and became a new country—the United States. At first, all this was too far away to make any difference to the Osage.

"But it soon began to matter. The United States started to grow. Americans began to move westward, seeking open land for homes and farms. They pushed many Indian tribes off their old lands. Some of these tribes came into the land of the Osage. My ancestors often fought these invaders.

"And then, in 1803, the American President, Thomas Jefferson, bought the Louisiana Territory from France. The land of the Osage now belonged to the United States. Many Americans began to come here.

"To the Osage, these people were worse enemies than the Indian invaders. They spoiled the land and drove the animals away. There was often trouble between the settlers and the Osage.

"The United States government offered the Osage money and other things to give up part of their land. They were to live at peace with the settlers and other Indians. The Osage knew they had to agree or the United States would send soldiers against them. In 1808, they signed a treaty. They gave up what is now most of the state of Missouri.

"Several more times the Osage were asked to give up land. By 1870, all the Osage lived on a big reservation in Oklahoma. The herds of buffalo they had hunted were gone—killed off by American hunters. The Osage now lived in log cabins and raised some crops. Most of the people were poor.

"Then, in 1897, oil was discovered on the Osage reservation! For a time, most of the Osage were wealthy. But many of them were tricked and cheated out of their wealth."

The rancher paused for a moment. He looked about at the rolling, grassy plain. "In 1907, the Osage reservation was made a county of the state of Oklahoma—Osage County. Most Osage still live here. They have farms and businesses. They live in much the same way as the other folks in Oklahoma."

He paused again, and grinned. "But, we're living on the same land our ancestors lived and hunted on hundreds of years ago. That's more than most Americans can say!"

The Pomo

People of California

The Pomo people lived on the west coast of
North America, just north of what is now San
Francisco Bay, California. A few hundred
years ago there were about eight thousand
Pomo. Some lived along the seacoast, others
by rivers or lakes, farther inland.

The climate in this land is mild all year
long. Near the coast lie forests of giant
redwood trees. Farther inland are grassy
valleys and forests of oak.

The Pomo led an easy life, for there was
always plenty of food. They hunted the birds
and animals of the forest. They fished in the
Pacific Ocean and in lakes and rivers. And
they gathered acorns, berries, and other wild
plant food.

The Pomo had many small villages. Each
village had a headman who saw that religious
ceremonies were held and that children were
taught the proper way of life. He also
entertained visitors and kept peace among the
villagers.

Tribes living near the Pomo were the Yuki,
Maidu, Wintun, Miwok, and Patwin. All these
people lived much like the Pomo.

The Ash Ghosts

The little girl was frightened. She sat huddled as close as she could to her mother. They were alone in the dark house. And soon, the Ash Ghosts would come!

Most of the time, life in the village was uneventful. All the days were much alike. The girl's father hunted or fished. Or, he might stay at home to make a weapon or a tool that was needed. The girl's mother spent a great deal of time gathering wild plants to eat. Or, she might spend the day weaving a basket. At night, families visited with each other. Then, the old people told stories of Coyote, the Trickster.

But today had been different! It was the time of the Ghost Ceremony. That afternoon, both the ordinary ghosts and the Ash Ghosts had danced through the village! The ordinary ghosts wore leaves and feathers on their heads. Their bodies were covered with paint.

The Ash Ghosts wore only a few feathers on their heads and a veil of leaves to cover their faces. They, too, had painted their bodies from head to foot. In their hands they carried their badge of office—a crooked stick, with one end carved to look like the head of a bird.

Now, it was after sunset. The village lay in darkness. The girl knew that all the women, girls, and small boys were hiding in their houses. All the men and older boys were at the big dance house. No women and children would be allowed there tonight.

A deep, booming *buroom-buroom-buroom* came from the dance house. The men were stamping on the foot drum—a hollow log placed over a shallow pit.

Suddenly the booming stopped. For a time, the village was silent. Then came another sound—a loud, long whistling moan!

"What is that?" squeaked the girl.

"The voice of the dead," whispered her mother.

The girl stiffened in fear and clutched at her mother's bark apron. She could hear sounds outside the house! Someone was scurrying about. She could see flickers of light. The Ash Ghosts!

The men playing the parts of the Ash Ghosts moved quickly through the village. Their painted bodies were smeared with ashes. Masks of leaves hid their faces. Some of them carried torches. The men peered into some of the houses, shaking their rattles at the frightened women and children. Then they entered the dance house.

In the dance house, some boys were being initiated into the secret society to which all the men belonged. The boys lay face down, in a row, on the floor. An old man had scratched each boy's back with a sharp piece of shell, causing blood to flow. This was done to remind the frightened boys that pain and fear are a part of life.

The Ash Ghosts were both clowns and magicians. They danced about, shaking their rattles. They put flaming torches into their mouths. And they picked up glowing coals with their bare hands!

Then they grabbed two boys who had sometimes been bad. Picking the boys up, they tossed them back and forth through the

flames of the fire to frighten them! The Ash Ghosts then spoke seriously to all the boys. They told them they must behave and respect older people.

After that, the headman of the village spoke. He told about the laws of life and the way young people should live. The best kind of person, he told the boys, is a hard worker who is kind to everyone and does things to help the whole village. Each boy, he said, should try to be this kind of person.

Now, the boys had become men. They joined in the dance that ended the ceremony.

The next day, the life of the village went on as it had before. The people went about the important business of finding food. The Ash Ghosts were gone. They would return when the next great ceremony took place.

Pomo ways

In northern California, where the Pomo lived, the climate is usually mild all year. So the Pomo people didn't wear much clothing.

Pomo women usually wore two aprons. One was narrow and worn in front. The other was larger and worn in back. Women who lived near a lake or river usually made their aprons out of rushes that grew along the shore. In villages near the redwood forests, aprons were generally made of redwood bark. Sometimes, though, the women wore a deerskin skirt.

Most of the time, Pomo men wore nothing at all. When they did, it was just a strip of deerskin around the waist. But on chilly nights or cool, rainy days, men and women wrapped themselves in warm, thick robes made of strips of rabbit skin woven together.

Pomo men and women did, however, dress up for special occasions. Their dress clothes were very colorful. They had headbands made from the orange and black feathers of the flicker. Skirts were made from the feathers of the turkey vulture. Women also wore necklaces made of shell, stone, and bone beads. Both men and women had their ears pierced. In the holes in the ear lobes they put long bone rods with tufts of bright feathers at each end. The men wore a similar rod in the nose. The men also painted their faces and the bare parts of their bodies with designs in black, red, and white.

The Pomo lived in small villages of about two hundred people. There was no wall around a Pomo village, and there were no

The Pomo Indians enjoyed playing games. These are pieces for two of the games they played.

Pomo men usually spent most of their spare time in a sweathouse. This place was like a club for them. They talked, played games, and even slept there.

streets. The houses were built wherever people felt like putting them.

The kind of houses the Pomo built depended upon where a village was located. Near a redwood forest, the houses were made of redwood bark. They were very simple houses. First, a pole was stuck in the ground. Then, long pieces of bark were leaned on a slant all around the pole. Only one family of four or five people lived in such a house.

The Pomo who lived near a lake or river made larger, dome-shaped houses. First, they stuck a number of thin poles into the ground to form a circle. They bent the tops of the poles in toward each other and tied them together. This framework was then covered with bundles of dried grass or dried rushes. Two or three families lived in such a house.

In every Pomo village there was a dance house. This was a large circular building, as much as sixty feet (18 meters) across. It was simply a round pit dug in the ground and covered over with a dome-shaped roof of earth and dried grass. It was used for special religious ceremonies.

Every Pomo village had at least one sweathouse. This was just like the dance house, only smaller. Men and boys usually took a sweat bath every day.

One of the most important Pomo foods was acorns. Acorns are the nuts of oak trees. We don't eat them because they are bitter and poisonous. But the Pomo knew how to take out the bitterness and poison.

In autumn, when oak trees are filled with acorns, each Pomo village held a great harvest. Men and boys climbed the trees to

After shelling acorns, the Pomo women used stones to grind the nuts into powder. The powder was then spread out in a shallow sand pit. Next, they poured hot water over the powder. This took out the poison and left a sticky dough.

shake down the acorns. The women and girls gathered them and put them into baskets. Enormous amounts of acorns were gathered and stored away.

The Pomo also ate many other kinds of plant food. They gathered berries and the roots of wild vegetables. They were fond of the young, tender leaves and stems of many plants. They also ate ground-up grass seed.

There were deer, rabbits, and many kinds of birds in Pomo country. Men caught birds and small animals in traps. They shot larger animals with arrows. Meat was broiled over a low fire. Some was cut in strips and dried in the sun. Then it was stored until needed.

There were also fish in the many streams. Men usually used nets to catch fish. Fish, too, was either broiled or dried and stored.

Pomo people often ate such things as boiled and roasted caterpillars, grasshoppers, and worms. These may not sound very good to you. But if you had been a Pomo child, you would have enjoyed them!

Acorn dough was mixed with water to make a paste. The paste was then put into a basket. The women cooked the paste by dropping hot stones, heated in a fire, into the basket. The result was a tasteless pudding.

Pomo women wove some of the most beautiful baskets in the world. They used the baskets to cook in and to keep things in.

The troubles of Coyote

A Pomo legend

There was a time when the world had no creatures living on it. So Coyote made some people out of rocks. He put the people into valleys to live. Then Coyote made all the different kinds of animals. He put them onto mountains to live. He put all the birds on one mountain. He sent all the furry creatures to another mountain. The lizards went onto a third mountain. And he put all the snakes onto a fourth mountain.

Coyote was pleased with most of the creatures he had made. But as he watched the people, he became angry. He had wanted people to live in peace. He had meant them to spend their time catching fish and gathering seeds to eat. Instead, they were often at war and doing bad things to each other. So Coyote sent a great flood into the valleys. All the people drowned.

Now the valleys were empty. So Coyote made new people and put them into the valleys to live. But these people were no better than the first ones. Again Coyote became angry. He sent a raging fire to kill all the second people.

The fire also burned the mountains. Most of the lizards and snakes were roasted. Coyote was hungry. So he ate the lizards and snakes.

After eating, he was very thirsty. He searched for days until he found water. He drank so much water that he swelled up. For four days he was dreadfully sick. Finally, Bullfrog came to his aid. With a stone knife, Bullfrog cut a hole in Coyote. All the water ran out of Coyote and formed a great lake.

Now Coyote made some more people. But these people were bad, too. The angry Coyote sent a whirlwind to kill them. The whirlwind also blew among the mountains. It blew the animals living on the mountains into all parts of the world. This is why you now find all kinds of animals everywhere.

Then Coyote made a fourth kind of people. But these people were just as bad as the others. So Coyote sent ice and snow to freeze them to death.

Finally, Coyote made a fifth kind of people. Most of them went to live near the big lake that had been made when Bullfrog opened up Coyote to let the water out. They stayed at peace. They lived the way Coyote wanted them to. They were The People—The Pomo.

Gold and destruction

The art teacher was showing her students how to weave a basket.

"There," she said as she finished. "Not bad. But my great-grandmother would have done better. She was a Pomo, and Pomo women made the most beautiful baskets in the world. But no one knows how to make baskets quite like them anymore."

"Why not?" asked a student.

"Because the Pomo have forgotten most of their old ways," said the teacher, sadly. "Pomo people have probably lived in California for as long as nine thousand years. In all that time, their way of life hardly changed at all. But then, less than two hundred years ago, things began to change."

"What happened?" another student asked.

"We met white people for the first time. They were Russians. They came here in 1808. A few years later, the Spanish, and then the Mexicans came. A mission was built at Sonoma. Cattle ranchers came into part of

The discovery of gold in California ended the Pomo way of life forever. As shown in this old print, the gold miners, settlers, and Chinese workers drove the Pomo and other Indians off the land.

our land. Then, in 1848, California became part of the United States.

"In that very same year, gold was discovered in California. Thousands of people rushed to the gold fields. At first, we were not bothered because there was no gold around here. But before long, settlers moved in. They took our land. They cut down the trees to make room for farms and ranches. Without the trees, there were no acorns.

"The settlers also killed off the animals of the forest. Soon, there wasn't enough food for the Pomo. Many of my people starved or died of diseases brought by the settlers. There were fewer and fewer Pomo.

"The white people looked upon the Pomo as savages. They even hunted them, like animals. They did not understand the Pomo way of life—that the Pomo were content and happy and didn't need to live in any other way. The Pomo had always been peaceful, so they didn't try to fight. To stay alive, many of the Pomo worked for the settlers. The white people were glad to hire them, because they didn't have to pay them much!

"Before the settlers came, there were about eight thousand Pomo. Today, there are only about a thousand. Most of the Pomo live on land that belongs to the government. Pomo children go to school in nearby towns. Most Pomo men are farmers."

The art teacher sighed. "So, the Pomo way of life is gone. I'm part Pomo, but I don't know much about how my ancestors did things." She looked sadly at the basket she had made. "I know I can't make the beautiful baskets Pomo women used to make!"

The Cherokee

People of the Southeastern Mountains

When Columbus reached America, the Cherokee were a large, powerful nation of about twenty thousand people. They lived in some eighty towns in what are now the states of Virginia, North and South Carolina, Georgia, Tennessee, and Alabama.

The Cherokee lived in a land of high mountains. Thick forests covered the land. Birds and other animals were everywhere. The Cherokee got much of their food by hunting and fishing. But they were also farmers. They grew several kinds of corn, as well as other food plants.

The Cherokee called themselves *Ani'Yun-wiya,* or "Real People." Other tribes knew them as "People of the Cave Country." The name *Cherokee* may come from the Creek word *tciloki,* meaning "people of a different speech."

Tribes closest to the Cherokee included the Creek, Chickasaw, Yuchi, and Tuscarora. A little to the north were the lands of the Shawnee and the Delaware. The Cherokee were often at war with one or more of these other tribes.

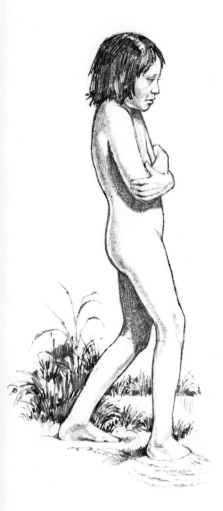

A Cherokee holiday

Tree Climber stood on the riverbank with his mother and father and all the other people of the town. His mother held his little sister, The Pretty One, in her arms.

Tree Climber's father, Looks-to-the-Moon, gave the boy a little nudge. Taking a deep breath, Tree Climber walked with his parents down the bank and into the water. He waded out into the river until the water was nearly up to his chest. The water was bitterly cold, for it was early springtime. But Tree Climber gritted his teeth and did what he had to do.

Facing east, toward the Sun, the Creator, Tree Climber ducked completely underwater seven times. His parents and everyone else did the same thing. The Pretty One cried a bit each time she was dipped into the water. Usually, dipping in cold water was a way to punish children who had been bad. But today, it was part of an important religious ceremony—the Festival of the First New Moon of Spring.

The ceremonies had started the night before, when the thin curve of the new spring moon appeared in the sky. The women started the festival with the Friendship Dance. The dance lasted until the moon set.

Just after dawn, everyone hurried to the temple in the center of the town. This building stood on a large, flat-topped mound. The mound had been built long ago. People had piled up thousands of basketsful of earth into a great mound with slanting sides. Logs, placed lengthwise one above the other, formed stairs leading to the top.

The temple at the top of the mound had seven sides and a dome-shaped roof. A big building, it could hold all of the nearly five hundred people of the town. Inside the temple, three rows of benches, one above the other, ran around the walls. Seven stout posts, arranged in a wide circle, supported the roof. There was a second row of posts inside these, and a thick center post.

The seven sides of the temple stood for the seven clans, or family groups, of the tribe. The number seven was very important to Tree Climber's people. The Festival of the First New Moon of Spring was one of seven religious holidays. Tree Climber knew there were seven directions—north, south, east, west, above, below, and "here in the center." He also believed that there were seven heavens in the sky.

When everyone was inside the temple, the chief known as the White Chief, who was also the high priest, brought out the sacred crystal, which looked like a piece of glass. The people believed that the sacred crystal had the power to show the future. The priest stared into the crystal for a long time. Everyone waited silently. Finally, the priest announced that the corn crop would be good.

After that, everyone had gone to the river. Now, Tree Climber came out of the water, rubbing himself to warm up. His parents wrapped deerskin capes around their shoulders, as did many of the other grown-ups. Tree Climber's mother tucked The Pretty One under her cape.

Tree Climber was hungry. No one had eaten since yesterday. And there would be no

food until the great feast tonight. He decided
to find some of his brothers and play war.

Tree Climber had a great many brothers
and sisters—hundreds of them, in fact. For
every child who belonged to his clan was
counted as a brother or sister. Tree Climber
and The Pretty One both belonged to the Bird
clan. This was their mother's clan. Their
father belonged to the Deer clan, the same
clan *his* mother belonged to. When Tree
Climber and The Pretty One grew up and
married, they would marry someone from
either the Wolf or the Long-Hair clan, the
clans of their two grandfathers.

Beautiful turkey-feather capes such as this one were made by Cherokee women. Such capes were usually worn only for special occasions.

The town that Tree Climber and The Pretty One lived in was only one of many towns in the land of the Real People. Like all the other towns, it had two chiefs. The chief known as the Red Chief was in charge of war and games. He also represented the town when it was necessary to meet with other tribes. The White Chief was in charge of farming, religious ceremonies, and the making of laws.

The Red Chief was a young man. He had been chosen because of his many deeds of bravery and his skill as a warrior. The White Chief was an older man. He had been picked because he was well-liked by everyone in the town. He was always good-natured, patient, and calm. The people called him "The Most Beloved Man."

Tree Climber liked and respected the White Chief. But he wanted to be the Red Chief some day! He often thought about being a brave warrior, like his father and like his mother's two brothers. War was very important to Tree Climber's people. The boy knew he could never truly be a man until he had fought bravely against his tribe's enemies.

This was why groups of young men often went forth to raid an enemy town. A woman known as the "Honored Woman," or "War Woman," often went with them. She did not fight, but she did tasks for the warriors and gave them advice. She also decided the fate of prisoners. She might decide that the prisoners should be adopted into the tribe. Or, she might decide they should be killed.

Tree Climber played war with some of his brothers for awhile. Later, he went into the woods with his mother to look for wild plant roots the family could eat. Time passed slowly for him. He was getting hungrier and hungrier!

Just before the sun set, everyone went back to the temple. A sacred fire always burned in the center of the temple. Now, the priest placed some tobacco flowers and a deer's tongue in the flames. As these things burned, the people believed that the rising smoke carried their prayers to the Creator, the Sun.

After this, the people feasted. Then they danced in the big open square at the base of the temple mound. Everyone danced until it was nearly morning.

The holiday had been a joyous one. The people were thankful for the coming of spring. They were certain that the corn crop would be a good one this year.

Cherokee ways

A Cherokee child usually had plenty of good food to eat. In summer, there might be a bubbling pot of corn and beans, together with broiled fish. In winter, there might be freshly baked, crunchy cornbread and smoked deer meat.

But in early spring, before the first crops were ripe, food was sometimes scarce. Then the Cherokee would eat just about anything they could find—such as bird's eggs, crayfish, turtles, and frogs.

The Cherokee were good farmers. Each family had a large garden next to their house. In spring and summer, everyone worked to raise crops. They grew corn, beans, squash, and pumpkins, as well as sunflowers, grown for their tasty seeds.

Corn was the most important crop. The Cherokee grew three kinds. One kind was eaten roasted. Another kind was boiled with vegetables. The third kind was ground into flour and used to make cornbread.

There was plenty of wild plant food in the land of the Cherokee, too. Women and children gathered crab apples, persimmons, berries, grapes, cherries, mushrooms, and plant roots. In the autumn, they looked for walnuts, chestnuts, and hickory nuts.

Cherokee men often fished with a hook and line. They also speared fish and caught them in traps.

The Cherokee also had a way of catching a great many fish at one time. They mashed up the roots of a certain plant. When they threw the mixture into the water, it "knocked out"

Cherokee women made flour from corn kernels as well as from sunflower seeds. They put the dried kernels or seeds into a hollow log. Then they crushed them by pounding them with a long, carved pole.

all the nearby fish. The fish then floated to the surface and the men scooped them out of the water!

In late autumn and winter, Cherokee families, except for very old people, left their village from time to time. They would camp in the woods while the men hunted.

The Cherokee mainly hunted deer, which they shot with arrows. To hunt birds and small animals, hunters used a blowgun. This weapon, made from the hollowed-out stem of a cane plant, shot small darts.

A Cherokee family had both a main house and a small house used during cold weather. The family ate and slept in the main house most of the time.

The Cherokee held religious dances and ceremonies in front of the town's temple mound. The Green Corn Dance gave thanks for a good corn crop.

A Cherokee family had two houses—a main house and a smaller winter house. Near their houses, each family had a garden in which they grew corn and other food plants.

The Cherokee played the game now called lacrosse. It was played with a small ball made of deerskin and stuffed with hair or moss.

The players had two short sticks. Each stick had a net on the end. Players used the sticks to try to take the ball to the goal.

For the Cherokee, this game was like a battle. The players used their sticks as clubs and often hurt one another. If a man didn't play hard enough, the women might beat him with whips!

The walls of the main house were made of poles stuck into the ground side by side to form a rectangle. Long, stiff stems of the cane plant were then woven in and out, lengthwise, among the poles. This made a sort of screen that was then smeared with wet clay. The clay dried stiff and white, much like plaster.

The sloping roof was made of poles covered with large pieces of chestnut tree bark. An opening in the roof let smoke out.

In the middle of the floor was a shallow pit for a cooking fire. A large, flat stone was always kept next to the fire pit. When the stone was heated on the fire, cornbread could be baked on it. The family stored food, tools, and other belongings against one wall. The beds, which were low platforms, were arranged against the other walls.

The family's other house was used for sleeping in winter or on cold nights. It was also used for taking sweat baths.

This house was small, low, and partly underground. The cone-shaped roof was made of poles covered with earth. There were beds and a fire pit in the cold-weather house. In cold weather, the fire was kept burning brightly all day. At night, it was allowed to almost go out. The little house would be warm as toast. But it was always smoky. The only way to let smoke out was to pull aside the skin that covered the entrance.

Most Cherokee clothing was made from deerskin. In the hot southern summers, a Cherokee man usually wore only a deerskin breechclout. Women wore a short skirt of deerskin. Everyone usually went barefoot.

In cold weather, or when hunting in the woods, men wore a sleeveless shirt, leggings, and moccasins. The moccasins were like short boots. Women also wore such moccasins in winter. And women covered their shoulders with a short deerskin cape.

For special occasions, Cherokee men and women might wear a cape made of turkey feathers. Women made the capes by sewing feathers between narrow strips of bark. They then sewed all the strips together. Brightly colored feathers of other birds were sewn onto the capes as decoration. Not only was such a cape beautiful, it was also lighter than a skin cape and just as warm.

Cherokee lacrosse sticks

Cherokee writing

For thousands of years, the Cherokee, like most other Indians of North and South America, had no way of writing. But in 1821, a Cherokee man known as Sequoyah (sih KWOY uh) invented a way of writing the Cherokee language.

Sequoyah did this without knowing how to read or write! He had no idea how letters were used to make words. He didn't even know what an alphabet was. But he realized that every Cherokee word was made up of several different sounds. He found there were about eighty-five different sounds in the Cherokee language. So, he made up a symbol for each sound. By putting the right symbols together, he could write any Cherokee word.

For example, in Cherokee, Sequoyah's name, which means "Sparrow," was made up of the four sounds chee ss kwah yah. So it is written with these four symbols:

$$\text{ⁱⁱⁱⁱ}$$

The artist who illustrated the Cherokee legend that starts on the next page is part Cherokee. His Cherokee name, *Yah-nah-sah*, means "Buffalo." He signed his art with the Cherokee symbols for these three sounds.

Here are some words as they are written with Sequoyah's symbols, and as they are spoken in Cherokee.

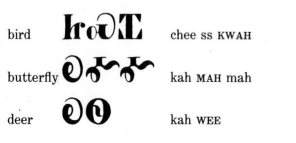

bird		chee ss KWAH
butterfly		kah MAH mah
deer		kah WEE

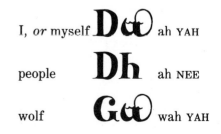

I, *or* myself		ah YAH
people		ah NEE
wolf		wah YAH

The first fire

A Cherokee legend

When the world was new, there was no fire. All the land was cold. The animals suffered terribly. But the Thunders who lived in heaven took pity and sent a bolt of lightning to the earth. The lightning struck the bottom of a dead, hollow tree that stood on an island. The tree began to burn.

The animals saw smoke curling up out of the top of the tree, and knew fire was there. They held a council to decide how they might get some fire. Every animal that could fly or swim offered to go to the island and bring back fire. Finally, the animals decided Raven should go. He was big and strong and should have no trouble.

Raven flew to the island and landed on the top of the tree. But as he sat there trying to decide how to get the fire, a breeze sprang up. The flames rose and scorched all of Raven's feathers. This is why all ravens are black. Frightened by the heat and smoke, Raven flew back without fire.

Next to try was the little Screech Owl. He flew to the island and perched on the hollow tree. But as he looked down into the fire, a blast of hot air shot up. The heat nearly blinded him. He managed to fly back to the council, but could not see well after that. This is why a screech owl's eyes are red and why he blinks when he looks into light.

The animals of the council then decided to send two animals. The Hoot Owl and Horned Owl flew there together. But by this time, the

whole tree was burning fiercely. The smoke
nearly blinded the two owls, and drifting
ashes made white rings around their eyes.
The owls had to come back without fire. No
matter how hard they rubbed their eyes, they
could not get rid of the white rings. And this
is why they still have white rings around
their eyes.

The birds had had enough. But the little
snake we call Black Racer said he would go.
He was a good swimmer and had no trouble
reaching the island. When he got there, he
crawled through the grass to the tree.

The little snake crawled into a small hole at
the bottom of the tree. But there was so
much smoke that he could not see anything,
and the hot ashes burned him. He twisted and
turned to escape the heat. Finally, he found

the hole again. He crawled out. But he had
been scorched black, as he is today. And ever
since then, the black racer twists and turns
quickly as he crawls, as if trying to get out
of a tight, hot place.

Then, the big Blacksnake said he would try.
He swam to the island and climbed up the
outside of the tree. But when he poked his
head in at the top to see the fire, the smoke
choked him—and he fell down inside the tree!
Before he could climb out, he was scorched as
black as Black Racer. This is why he is called
blacksnake.

After this, none of the birds or snakes or
four-footed animals wanted to go near the
burning tree. But unless one of the animals
could get fire, the world would stay cold.

At last, Water Spider said she would go.

Now, she can run across the top of the water and even dive to the bottom. So she had no trouble getting to the island. But then she had to stop and think. How was she to bring fire back?

Then she had an idea. She quickly spun some silk and wove it into a tiny bowl. Then she tied the bowl to her back. Creeping to the tree, she reached out with one of her long arms and scooped a tiny, glowing coal out of the fire. She put the coal into the basket on her back.

Then she ran quickly back across the water to the waiting animals. And to this day, the big, black, red-striped water spider still carries a red bowl on her back. It is the one in which she brought fire to the world.

The trail of tears

The young man sat on a park bench. He was busily typing away on a portable typewriter he held on his lap. A young woman came and sat down beside him. She watched him with curiosity. Finally, she asked, "Are you a writer?"

He stopped typing and nodded. "Yes. I'm writing a book."

"What's it about?" she wanted to know.

"It's about my people, the Cherokee people," he told her. "I'm a full-blooded Cherokee. My book is going to tell the story of a Cherokee family during the last four hundred or so years."

"That sounds neat," she exclaimed. "Will you tell me a little about it?"

"Well," he said, "it begins when the Spanish explorer Hernando de Soto came into Cherokee territory. That was in 1540. He and his men were searching for gold. But when they found nothing, they left.

"About a hundred years later, Frenchmen came, and then Englishmen. They were fur traders. They traded guns, metal tools, and other things to the Cherokee for the skins of animals. The Cherokee came to depend on the traders for almost everything. They no longer knew how to make stone tools and other things their ancestors had made. Their way of life had changed.

"By the 1700's, English settlers were coming into Cherokee territory to build homes and farms. The Cherokee had to give up some of their land to these people. Then, in 1776, the American colonies went to war against

Great Britain to make America a free nation. The British asked the Cherokee to help them, and we did.

"When the Americans won the war, we ended up on the losing side. The American government made us give up a lot more land. But we did the best we could on the land we had left. Most of the Cherokee turned to farming or business.

"Thanks to one man, a Cherokee named Sequoyah (sih KWOY uh), nearly all the Cherokee could read and write in their own language. Sequoyah invented symbols for all the sounds in the Cherokee language, and so gave our people a way to write.

"By 1828, most of the Cherokee were well off. Some even owned big plantations and had slaves, just as many southern Americans did. We had formed a new nation, called the Cherokee nation, and a government that was a lot like the government of the United States. We even had a president. He was John Ross, one of the greatest leaders the Cherokee ever had. We had our own schools and our own newspaper."

The young writer shook his head angrily. "It seemed we were doing all the things the Americans wanted us to do," he said. "They always talked about educating the Indians and making them just like white people. But we quickly found out that a lot of Americans really didn't want that. What they wanted was our land!

"Even though the Cherokee land was protected by a treaty with the United States, it didn't matter. In 1830, the government passed a law forcing all the Indians in the

Sequoyah, a Cherokee man, could not read or write. But in 1821, after twelve years of work, he invented a way of writing the Cherokee language.

This is part of a page from a Cherokee newspaper of 1828. It is printed in both English and Cherokee.

southeast to move west across the Mississippi River, into what is now Oklahoma.

"In 1838, the government sent seven thousand soldiers to round up the Cherokee and put them into camps. The local white people stole our animals and burned our houses. But the worst was yet to come.

"In October, 1838, the soldiers began to force the Cherokee westward in groups of about a thousand. Most of the people were on foot. Winter struck while they were still traveling. They had to make their way through freezing rain, blizzards, and terrible cold. There wasn't enough food and there was no shelter.

"About four thousand people—almost one-fourth of all those who started out—died of cold or disease! Often, the people were not

In 1838, the United States government forced most Cherokee to leave their homes and move hundreds of miles west. Thousands died during the long, hard journey, known as The Trail of Tears.

even given time to bury their dead. To this day, we Cherokee still call that terrible journey the 'Trail of Tears.'

"But, not all the Cherokee left their beloved homeland. About a thousand managed to escape. They hid in the mountains of North Carolina. But it seemed hopeless. In time, surely, they would be caught and sent away like the others.

"But, with money these Cherokee had saved, a white trader, Colonel William Thomas, bought land for them. This was a clever trick! The land couldn't be taken from the Cherokee because it belonged to the white man.

"So today there are two groups of Cherokee. One group of more than five thousand still live on their land in North Carolina. They have their own factories, a lumber industry, and motels for tourists. During the summer, Cherokee actors, dancers and musicians put on a marvelous play. Called 'Unto These Hills.' It is the story of the Cherokee people.

"The other group of Cherokee live halfway across the nation, in Oklahoma. They also put on a play each summer. Their play is also about my people. It is called 'The Trail of Tears.'

"That's the background of my book," the young writer said proudly. "The history of my people! We were a great nation before any Europeans came to this country. We were a great nation when the government forced us to leave our homes. We've shown that we can come out on top in spite of all our troubles. We're proud of our history!"

The Blackfoot

Wanderers of the Great Plains

The Blackfoot included three tribes—the Siksika (SIHK sih kuh), the Kainah (KY nuh), or Blood, and the Piegan (pay GAN). Each tribe had the same language and customs.

About two hundred years ago, there were some fifteen thousand Blackfoot. They lived in small bands in an area that stretched from what is now northern Montana in the United States to central Alberta in Canada. This is the northern part of the Great Plains. There, buffalo roamed by the millions. The Blackfoot lived mainly off the buffalo.

The chief of each Blackfoot band was chosen by the people of the band. He was picked because he was brave and wise. He did not make laws or give orders. The people simply followed his advice.

Other tribes that lived on the plains near the Blackfoot were the Cree, the Assiniboin, the Atsina (also known as the Gros Ventre), and the Crow. These tribes had much the same way of life as the Blackfoot.

In the mountains to the west lived the Kutenai, the Flathead, and the Shoshone. The Blackfoot were often at war with one or another of their neighbors.

The winter camp

The valley wore a coat of gleaming white snow. The river that snaked through the valley was silent and still, covered with thick gray ice. The trees clustered along the riverbank seemed like bare skinny, black skeletons without their thick summer thatch of leaves. The valley, like the rest of the vast plains country, was held tight in the cold, hard, silent grip of winter.

But at one place beside the river there was noise and movement. In an open spot among the trees stood a dozen cone-shaped tepees. Blue smoke curled upward from the opening at the top of each tepee. A few figures moved among the tepees. Nearby, on the frozen river, a number of small figures raced about. This was a winter camp of a group of the people who called themselves Siksika—the "Black-Footed People."

During spring, summer, and most of autumn, the Blackfoot followed the great herds of buffalo across the plains. But in winter, terrible storms lashed the plains. With snow piled as high as a tall man's chest, travel was impossible. So in winter, the bands of "Black-Footed People" stayed in one place.

They made a camp in a valley, beside a river and among trees. The valley gave them some protection from the fierce winds that swept the plains. The trees, acting like a snow fence, kept snow from piling up around the tepees. The trees also provided plenty of firewood. And to get water, people chopped a hole in the ice on the river. On cold days, they huddled around the fires in their tepees.

Winter was a time for mending old things and making new ones. It was a time for telling stories or listening to them. But the people had work to do, too. They had to keep the fire burning in each tepee. Every day, the women went to gather armloads of tree branches. And if a family's supply of smoked meat and dried vegetables and berries was running low, they had to find more food.

A man stepped out of one of the tepees. He was warmly dressed in winter clothes made of thick buffalo hide, with the fur inside. He carried a bow and arrows and a pair of snowshoes. He was going hunting.

He planned to make his way through the woods along the river. With luck he might find an elk or a few deer not too far away. But he might have to search for several days, until he found some buffalo. In the summer, all the men of the band hunted buffalo together. But in winter, the men sometimes hunted alone.

If the man were lucky enough to find some buffalo, he would cover himself with a wolf skin. Then he'd creep slowly toward the buffalo. They would pay no attention to him because wolves could not harm them. When he was close enough, he'd kill one of the animals with an arrow.

As the man bent over to put on his snowshoes, he glanced toward the river. He looked to where the shouts and laughter of children resounded. His son and daughter were playing there, with the other children of the band.

The children played many different games on snow and ice. One favorite game was "hunting the buffalo." First, a group of girls slid down a snowy hill, each girl sitting on a large piece of buffalo hide. The girls played the part of the buffalo. The boys slid down after them, on sleds made of buffalo ribs. The boys played the hunters. When all the children were mixed up at the bottom of the hill, each boy tried to poke a girl in the stomach and shout, "I kill you now!"

But now the children played a sliding game on the icy river. A thin coat of snow made the ice good and slippery. The boys and girls ran and then let themselves slide. As they slid, they tried to see how many times they could shout "Man, it's sure true," before coming to a stop—or falling down.

The man smiled to see the children enjoying themselves. Then he started on his way. The snowshoes helped him to move quickly and easily over the snow.

In spite of the snow, the man knew it would soon be spring. Since the beginning of winter, he had kept track of the days by cutting notches on a stick. Before long the ice on the river would start to break up. The snow would begin to melt. Flocks of geese flying north would fill the air with their honking. Then it would be time to take down the tepees and move back to the plains.

Blackfoot ways

The most important and favorite food of the Blackfoot people was buffalo. They called it their "real food." After a good buffalo hunt, a man might eat five pounds (2.25 kilograms) of buffalo meat.

The Blackfoot ate nearly every part of a buffalo. Fresh meat was roasted or boiled. A soup was made from buffalo fat and blood mixed with wild berries. A kind of sausage was made by cleaning a piece of intestine, filling it with pieces of meat, and roasting it. Dried buffalo meat was pounded together with fat and chokecherries to make a hard, chewy food known as pemmican. Buffalo tongue, brains, and liver were all treats.

The Blackfoot also hunted antelope, deer, mountain sheep, and small animals for food and skins. But most would not eat birds or

Before they had horses, the Blackfoot used dogs to help them carry things. A bundle was tied on a flat basket between two poles. The two poles were tied together at one end and fastened to a harness on the dog's back. A big dog could drag seventy-five pounds (34 kilograms).

In the days when they had no horses, Blackfoot men would wear the skin of a wolf to hunt buffalo. The buffalo weren't afraid of wolves, so they paid no attention to the disguised hunters. The men could creep up close and kill a buffalo with arrows.

fish. And, unlike some tribes, they looked upon their dogs as friends and would only eat them to keep from starving.

The Blackfoot didn't grow any kind of food plant. But they did eat wild plants. The women and children used sharp sticks to dig up wild turnip roots and camass bulbs. They ate roots raw, roasted, or boiled. They also dried and stored them for winter. Then they used them in stews, with dried buffalo meat.

Berries and chokecherries were eaten raw or mixed into soups and stews. Many were dried to use in winter. When there were plenty of ripe, juicy berries, the Blackfoot often mashed them and drank the juice.

The Blackfoot usually ate two cooked meals a day, one in the morning and one in the evening. If they were moving camp, they might stop at noon to eat some dried buffalo meat, berries, or pemmican.

Like all Plains Indians, the Blackfoot were on the move most of the year. They had to

keep following the buffalo herds. Each
Blackfoot family had a cone-shaped tent
called a tepee. *Tepee* comes from the Sioux
word *tipi*, meaning "dwelling." This kind of
house, which was used by all the Plains
Indians, could be carried about and put up
and taken down easily.

When a hunting band reached a camping
place, the women put up the tepees. They
held up the tepees with poles that they
brought with them. The poles were the
trunks of slim young trees with all the bark
peeled off. The cover, made of a number of
buffalo skins, was then wrapped around the
poles and fastened in place.

Before the Plains Indians had horses,
tepees were not very big. The size of the
cover and the number of poles was limited by
the weight dogs could drag or carry. After
they got horses, the Indians made their
tepees larger. The average tepee was about
twelve to fifteen feet (3.6 to 4.5 meters) high

*A tepee cover was made by sewing a
number of buffalo skins together in a
half circle. This was done by an old
woman who knew how to do it. When
she was finished, she was given a feast
to pay her for her work.*

Blackfoot women always put up the family tepee. First, they tied the tops of four poles together. The bottoms of the poles were pushed into the ground to form a rectangle. Twelve more poles were leaned around the four poles to form a cone.

Next, the skin cover was stretched along another pole. This pole was lifted up and rested against the others. The cover was then pulled tight around all the poles and fastened in place.

Two other poles were pushed into the smoke flaps at the top of the tepee. The flaps were opened or closed by moving these poles.

Tepees were usually painted. Designs were animals or birds the tepee owner had seen in a dream. The top of the tepee was often painted black to stand for the sky at night. The bottom was painted red to stand for the earth.

and fifteen feet (4.5 m) across at the bottom. Two poles outside the tepee held the smoke flaps. By moving these poles, the smoke flaps could be adjusted to the wind, or closed if it rained or snowed.

The Blackfoot made their finest clothes from the skins of antelope or mountain sheep. They usually made their everyday clothes of deer or elk skins. During the hot summer

Only Plains Indians wore feather bonnets. And only a chief or a great warrior could wear one. This eagle-feather bonnet is the kind the Blackfoot wore. A Sioux bonnet had a long streamer of feathers.

days on the plains, the Blackfoot seldom wore much clothing. But, winters on the plains are often fiercely cold.

A very important piece of winter clothing was a warm buffalo robe. It was made of one large piece of skin with the fur left on. The side without fur was usually decorated with designs that were painted or made of colored porcupine quills sewn in place.

When the Plains Indians got horses, their way of life changed. They could travel faster, carry heavier loads, and hunt more easily. And war parties now rode horses when they went off to raid or to fight.

Sign language

The Indian tribes of the Plains did not all speak the same language. But these people often had to communicate with one another. So the Blackfoot and other tribes worked out a sign language to talk to each other.

Some of the signs used by the Plains Indians are shown below. In the picture, the children are making the sign for "friend."

Father: Touch the right side of your chest several times with your right fist.

Mother: Touch the left side of your chest several times with your right fist.

I: Point to yourself with your right thumb.

You: Point to person with your right thumb.

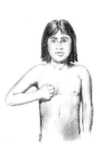

father   *I*

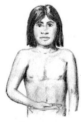

hungry   *dog*   *teepee*   *sleep*   *drink*

Thank you: Hold your hands chest high, palms facing out. Push your hands slowly toward the person you wish to thank, letting your hands curve downward.

Bird: Hold your hands at your shoulders, as shown. Move your hands up and down, like the flapping of a bird's wings.

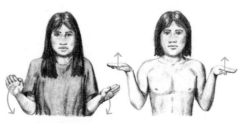

thank you   *bird*

How things were made

A Blackfoot legend

Long ago, in the beginning, there was
nothing but water. One day, Napi, Old Man,
decided to find out if there was anything
under the water. He sent Duck to dive down
into the water and look. But Duck did not
find anything. Old Man then sent Otter to
look. But Otter didn't find anything either.
Nor did Badger, when Old Man sent him.

Then Old Man sent Muskrat. Muskrat was
underwater for so long that Old Man thought
he must have drowned. But, finally,
Muskrat's head popped up out of the water.
In his paws he held a little lump of mud.

Old Man took the lump of mud and blew on
it. The mud began to swell up. It grew and
grew until it was the whole world.

Old Man began to walk about on the world.
He piled up rocks to make high mountains.
He made long gashes and deep holes in the
earth. These he filled with water to make
rivers and lakes. He made grass grow on the
plains and trees grow on the mountains and
along the rivers. He made all the different
kinds of birds and animals. Then he picked up
a lump of clay and made a wife for himself—
Old Woman.

Old Man and Old Woman decided to make
people. "I shall have the first say as to what
they will be like," said Old Man.

"Very well," agreed Old Woman, "but I
shall have the last say."

Old Man thought for a moment. Then he
said, "The people shall have eyes and a

mouth. These shall be straight up and down on their faces."

But Old Woman said, "Yes, the people shall have eyes and a mouth. But these will be placed crosswise in their faces." And that is how it was.

Next, Old Man said, "The people shall have ten fingers on each hand."

But Old Woman said, "Ten fingers on a

hand is too many. They will get in the way. The people shall have four fingers and a thumb on each hand." And so it was.

Finally, Old Man and Old Woman finished working out the way people should look. But they could not decide whether to let people live forever or to have them die.

Old Man saw some dried up buffalo droppings on the ground. Picking one of these up, he said, "I will throw this buffalo chip into the water. If it floats, people will die for four days. But then they will come back to life forever. But if it sinks, they will stay dead forever."

He threw the buffalo chip into the water, where it floated.

But Old Woman still had the last say. She picked up a stone. "I will throw this stone into the water," she said. "If it floats, people will die for only four days. But if it sinks, they will die forever."

She threw the stone into the water. It sank, meaning people would have to die and be dead forever. "It is better that way," said Old Woman. "If people lived forever, they would never feel sorry for one another."

After they were made, the people were cold and hungry. They didn't know what to do. So Old Man showed them where to find berries and how to dig for roots that were good to eat. He showed them how to make bows and arrows, and traps, deadfalls, and snares to catch the buffalo and other animals. And he showed them how to make animal skins into warm clothes.

Then Old Man knew his work was done. He climbed a mountain and disappeared.

The proud people

The door slammed. A small, angry boy burst into the house. His mother saw he was upset. "What's the matter, Bill?" she asked.

"Aw, the guys were teasing me about being a Blackfoot," he said. "They told me if I washed my feet they wouldn't be black anymore!"

His mother laughed. "I was teased like that, too. Don't let it bother you. Just tell them you're really a Siksika."

The boy looked puzzled. "I thought we were Blackfoot."

"We are. You see, Siksika means 'black-footed.' This was the name the Cree Indians gave to us—probably because our moccasins were blackened by prairie fires, or painted black.

"Long ago, we were probably one big tribe. At that time, our people lived in the forest to the East. Scientists think this tribe was slowly pushed out onto the plains. As the Europeans pushed other tribes out of their lands, these Indians pushed us out of ours. The Blackfoot reached the plains about 1720. Then they split up into three separate tribes —the Siksika, the Kainah, or Blood, and the Piegan. Today, people call all three tribes the Blackfoot."

"Did our tribe have horses when it was in the forest?" wondered the boy.

"No," said his mother. "Even after they reached the plains, the Blackfoot hunted and traveled on foot. There weren't any horses in North America until the Spanish explorer Hernando Cortez brought them into Mexico in

Horses were wealth to the Indians of the Plains. So, the tribes often stole horses from one another. This painting by Charles Russell shows Blackfoot warriors on their way back from a horse-stealing raid.

1519. After a while, Indians got hold of some horses and learned to breed them. The Blackfoot got horses and guns about 1740. And these changed their way of life.

"Traders from Canada came among the Blackfoot in 1780. They were the first white men the Blackfoot had ever seen. At that time, the Indians and the traders were friendly. But in 1804, when a group of Blackfoot met some Americans of the Lewis and Clark expedition, there was trouble. The Blackfoot tried to steal some horses from the Americans. One of the Americans stabbed an Indian and killed him.

"The Blackfoot began to look upon all

Curly Bear, a Blackfoot chief, lived more than sixty years ago. He is wearing the "dress-up" clothes that wealthy Plains Indians wore for special occasions.

white Americans as their enemies. They named them 'Long Knives.' For many years, the Blackfoot fought to keep all American traders out of their country. At this time, our people also raided the Crow, Shoshone, Flathead, and other tribes to get horses. We were a very warlike people.

"However, the United States government sent people to try to make friends with the Blackfoot. And in 1855, the Blackfoot signed a treaty. We agreed to let white people pass through our country, and even allowed a few to settle. Each year, the government gave us money, food, cloth, and other things.

"For a while, all was well. But as more and more white Americans settled on Blackfoot land, trouble started. Young Blackfoot warriors saw nothing wrong in going on horse-stealing raids against the white settlers, just as they did against other Indians. The raiders killed some white people and the whites killed some raiders.

"In January, 1870, a small force of United States soldiers attacked the winter camp of Chief Heavy Runner in Montana. They were after a few young braves who had killed a white man. It made no difference that this was a friendly Blackfoot band. The soldiers killed 173 men and women and took 140 women and children prisoner. Most Americans were horrified by this dreadful massacre. The Blackfoot saw that they were helpless against the army. So the horse raids soon stopped.

"In the following years, government workers tried to get the Blackfoot to become farmers. They warned us that the great herds of buffalo might soon disappear. And in time, this warning came true. Thousands of white hunters killed the buffalo just for the skins. By 1890, the great herds of buffalo had disappeared. Where there had been many millions, only a few hundred were left!

"This meant starvation for the Blackfoot and other Plains Indians. They had to depend upon the American and Canadian governments to give them food. Often, there wasn't enough. For a number of years, many Indians died of starvation.

"The Blackfoot way of life changed. Much of the land where we had hunted buffalo was now wild and empty. So we sold the land to the governments of the United States and Canada. We—the Siksika—and the Kainah settled on reservations in Canada. The Piegan kept a reservation in Montana. We could no longer hunt for a living, so we became farmers and ranchers. We gave up our skin tepees for wooden houses.

"At first, things went well. But in 1919, there was a dry summer. Most of the Blackfoot crop was lost. A terribly fierce winter followed. Thousands of cattle and horses died. Many of the Blackfoot were left with nothing. Once again, we had to depend upon the government for food and help.

"But with time, we recovered. Today, most of the Blackfoot still live on reservations, where they farm and raise cattle. But some, like our family, live and work in towns."

She put her arm about her son and hugged him close. "Bill," she said, "the next time your friends kid you, remember what I told you. You are a Blackfoot—a Siksika. And we are a proud people!"

The Arawak

People of the Caribbean Islands

The Arawak people lived in what is now known as the West Indies. These islands form a long chain that stretches from the tip of Florida to Venezuela in South America. They separate the Caribbean Sea from the rest of the Atlantic Ocean.

Most of the islands have grassy valleys and thick forests. Mountains rise on many of them. Even in winter, the weather is quite mild. Before the arrival of Columbus, more than a million Arawak lived in the West Indies. Some of their villages had as many as a thousand houses. The people raised many kinds of food plants on farms near their villages. Arawak men also hunted and fished.

Each Arawak village was ruled by a chief, or headman. The chief had a special house, ate special food, and wore special clothes and ornaments. He ruled like a king, with the power of life or death over his people. When a chief died, his oldest sister's oldest son became the new chief.

The Carib, a fierce, warlike people, also lived on some of the Caribbean islands. The Carib, who were cannibals, were a constant threat to the peaceful Arawak.

The giant birds

It was corn-planting time. The sun had just risen, but the field near the village was already dotted with women doing their planting.

One little girl squatted close to her mother, watching her work. The mother was squatting, too, jabbing holes in the ground with a pointed stick. After making a hole, she reached into the bag that hung from her shoulder. Scooping out four or five kernels of corn, she dropped them into the hole.

The field lay on a sloping hillside. It was a small field, surrounded by forest. Only a few years before, the field had been part of the forest. But the men had cleared the field by burning the trees.

That sort of thing was men's work. That, and hunting, fishing, and teaching children the ways of the tribe. The women planted the crops, cared for them, cooked the food, and made the pots and baskets the family needed. Only when it came time to harvest the crops did the men and women work together. The little girl would have giggled to think of a man cooking or a woman going hunting.

There was also another thing that only men did. They went on the long journeys to search for the soft, shiny, yellow rock that was made into pretty ornaments. The girl had often seen the village headman and other important people wearing such ornaments in their noses and ears. Of course, common people such as her parents didn't own gold ornaments.

Her mother planted the last kernels of corn and stood up. She and the girl walked through the field to the edge of the forest. They stopped at the foot of a large tree.

Now it was time for the little girl to do her work. She scrambled quickly up the tree trunk to a platform built among the higher branches. From there, she would watch for birds that might come flapping down to eat the kernels of corn her mother had just planted. There were other children on other platforms among the trees. If any birds appeared, all the children would shout and wave, to frighten them away.

"Be home before the sun is overhead," the girl's mother called. Then she started down the path through the trees to the village.

Standing on the platform, the girl could look through the trees to the ocean. She knew the land she lived on was surrounded by water. She also knew there were other islands not far away. People from her village often visited these islands by canoe, to trade. People of her tribe lived on many islands. But enemy people—especially the fierce Carib— also lived on some of the islands.

She didn't know if there were other lands far out on the water. For all she knew, the sea went on forever. Her father had told her how the sea came to be. It had happened long ago, when four brothers spilled water out of a magical container.

To the girl's people, the sea was part of their home. They even used it as a road to get to other parts of their island. They didn't like to travel on land. And so, canoes were very important to them. In fact, from where she stood, the girl could see two men from her village making a canoe.

The work had started some time ago. First, the men had killed a tree by burning a ring around the trunk. After a while, the leaves turned dry and brown, showing that the tree was dead. Now its wood would be dry and easy to work with.

The men had burned the ring deeper and deeper, until the tree tottered and fell. Then they trimmed off all the branches, so that only a smooth log remained. Now, with sharp stone tools they were chopping out the inside of the log.

An insect buzzed against the girl's cheek, tickling her. Brushing it away, she wondered what would be in the pepperpot for her to eat when she got home. Fish probably, for her father had gone fishing. The pepperpot, filled with water and vegetables, was always bubbling over a fire. Whatever her father brought home from fishing or hunting was usually added to the pot.

She yawned, and glanced toward the sea. Suddenly she froze. Her mouth opened wide in surprise.

Something was out there on the blue water—things such as she had never seen before. They looked like three giant birds sitting on the sea. Each one had a fat, dark body and enormous white wings. She stared in wonder. What could they be?

The little girl did not know that her world was about to change. The things that looked to her like giant birds were three ships from Spain. Aboard one of the ships, Christopher Columbus peered eagerly toward the low, green island. The people of Europe had "discovered" the New World.

Arawak women ground manioc roots into a soft pulp. To take out the poisonous juice, they put the pulp into a long tube of twisted cotton that had a loop at each end. The top loop was slipped over a tree branch. A pole was put into the bottom loop. Jumping up and down on the pole stretched the tube and squeezed out the juice.

The Arawak used the pulp of manioc roots to make lumpy cakes. They baked these cakes on stones set over a fire.

Arawak houses were made of dried leaves and the stems of cane plants. The house shown is the kind common people lived in. Manioc cakes are drying on the roof.

Arawak ways

If you have ever eaten tapioca pudding, you have eaten one of the main foods of the Arawak people. Tapioca is made from the root of the manioc (MAN ee ahk) plant. But the Arawak did not make tapioca into a sweet pudding. They made it into cakes.

The Arawak also grew potatoes, beans, peppers, and peanuts. Most of the time these foods were mixed with water and with juice squeezed from manioc roots. This mixture was used to make a kind of soup.

The soup was made in a pot that was always kept boiling over a fire. This pot was known as the pepperpot. As soup was eaten, new foods were put into the pepperpot. So there was always plenty of soup.

There was also meat in the pepperpot soup.

The Arawak people slept in a kind of hanging bed now called a hammock. Spanish explorers had never seen such beds. They took the idea from the Arawak and began to use these beds on ships.

Arawak canoes were hollowed-out logs.
Canoes were important to the Arawak, who
used them for fishing and to travel to other
islands.

A remora is a large fish
that has an odd, sticky
patch on its head. The
Arawak trained these fish
to catch turtles. They
fastened a line to the fish.
When the fish stuck itself
to a turtle, both animals
were pulled up.

Arawak men hunted birds and animals, which
they killed with clubs. The main kind of meat
came from an animal we call a hutia (hoo TEE
uh). A hutia looks much like a squirrel with a
short, skinny tail.

Arawak men also caught fish with hook and
line, with nets, or by spearing them. Meat
and seafood was either roasted over a fire or
boiled in the pepperpot.

Because the weather is always warm where
they lived, Arawak people really needed no
clothing. Men and children seldom wore
anything at all. Married women wore only a
sort of apron made of grass, leaves, or
twisted cotton. The wife of a chief might
wear an apron that reached down to her
ankles. The wife of a common man wore a
much shorter apron.

Although they wore few clothes, Arawak
men and women liked ornaments, especially
necklaces and bracelets. The beads of most
necklaces were made of stone, bone, clay, or
seashells. Necklaces were among an Arawak

The Arawak carved fishhooks out of snail shells.

family's most prized possessions. Parents handed these down to their children, usually when the children got married.

Arawak men and women wore bracelets on their arms and legs. The bracelets were made of beads or twisted cotton. Men and women often wore earrings. And they might also wear an ornament that hung from a hole in their nose.

The Arawak knew where to find gold on their islands. They made the gold into ornaments. Usually, only the chiefs and nobles, or members of their families, wore gold ornaments. Chiefs wore special necklaces made of gold mixed with copper. Sometimes, they wore crowns made of gold that had been hammered until the gold was very thin.

Arawak women and men often painted their bodies for special occasions such as holidays. Men usually painted themselves red. Women used white paint. For holidays and dances, people also stuck feathers in their hair and put on masks made of wood or seashell.

The kind of house an Arawak family lived in depended on who they were. A chief's house did not look like the houses the common people lived in. It was larger and shaped differently.

The houses of common people were round and had a cone-shaped, pointed roof. These houses were made from the stems of cane and rattan plants. A cane stem is like a bamboo pole. Rattan is a kind of palm tree.

The floor of a house was simply the bare ground. Stools made of stone or carved wood were the only furniture. People slept in hammocks that hung from the walls. The hammocks looked like nets made of twisted cotton. Baskets hung from the roof. Weapons and other belongings leaned against the walls. The house had a low doorway and sometimes a number of small windows. Several families lived in such a house.

A chief's house was built of the same things as a commoner's house. But a chief's house was bigger and was shaped like a rectangle. The roof had two slanting sides. Only the chief's family lived in this house—but a chief might have several wives and lots of children!

Arawak hunters built pens in which to catch animals called hutias. They used dogs and torches to scare the hutias into the pens.

The First People

An Arawak legend

Long, long ago, there was nothing on the earth. There were no trees or animals or stones or water. There was nothing.

At that time, the First People lived in a great cave in a mountainside. They never went out during the daytime. Sometimes, however, a few people crept out at night to look around. And that is how things came onto the earth. For the sun caught some of the people outside the cave and turned them into trees. Others were turned into stones. And some became animals.

A man named Guagugiana lived in the cave. He had a very good friend named Giadruvava. One night, Guagugiana became sick. His friend Giadruvava left the cave to look for a certain kind of plant that could cure people. But, alas, he was so busy looking for the plant he did not notice the sun coming up. The sun caught him and turned him into a bird. And that is the bird that now sings so sadly in the morning.

Guagugiana got well. But he was filled with sadness over the loss of his friend. Angrily, he decided to defy the sun and go out into the world, "Who will come with me?" he called.

But none of the other men stirred. They were all afraid.

So Guagugiana turned to the women. "The men are all cowards!" he shouted. "Leave them! Come with me into the world, where we will find many good things!"

The women were willing, so off they went with Guagugiana. Many of them had babies, whom they carried with them.

Guagugiana took the women far away. He stayed with them for a while, but he was bothered by the crying of the babies. So he took all the babies and carried them away to a pond. There, he left them.

The poor babies lay beside the pond, crying "Milk! Milk!" Finally, the sun took pity on them and turned them into the first frogs. This is why frogs sit beside the water and make a noise that sounds as if they are begging for something over and over again.

After a while, the men who had stayed behind in the cave came out to look for the women. They could not find them. "What shall we do?" the men asked one another. "We shall have no wives!"

But then the men discovered some strange creatures living in the trees in a forest. The creatures had arms, legs, and heads, but no faces. They were neither male nor female. So the men begged some woodpeckers to carve faces on the creatures and make them into women. With their sharp bills, the clever woodpeckers pecked away. They soon gave the creatures the bodies and faces of women. Then the men married the women and began to build a village.

There was no sea in the world at that time. But this is how the sea came to be. A man named Giaia had an argument with his son. The son became angry and tried to kill his father. In order to defend himself, Giaia had to kill his son.

Sadly, he put the young man's bones into a gourd full of drinking water. He then hung the gourd inside his house. A few days later, he took the gourd down and looked into it. Lo and behold, the bones had turned into fish that were swimming about in the water! Wondering if the fish were good to eat, he took some of them out and cooked them. When he tasted the fish, he found that they were very good.

Now there were four brothers living nearby. They had seen Giaia eating the fish. They, too, wondered how the fish tasted. So, one day when Giaia was away, the four brothers crept into his house. They took some fish out of the gourd and cooked them. Then they sat down to eat.

But, as they were eating, they heard sounds that made them think Giaia was returning. Hastily, they hung up the gourd and scampered out of the hut.

But they had not hung up the gourd properly. It fell to the ground and water dripped out of it. The drip became a trickle. Soon, the trickle grew into a stream. Then the stream became a torrent!

The water, filled with fish, rushed out of the door of Giaia's house. It flowed across the countryside. It swept around in a great circle and met itself again. It spread out in all directions. The place where the First People lived became an island. And this is how the sea came to be.

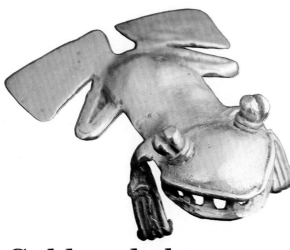

An Arawak artist made this gold frog. It was hung from a string worn around a person's neck.

Gold and slavery

The teacher pointed to a tiny spot on the big wall map. "Columbus landed here, about noon, on October 12, 1492. The Arawak called this island *Guanahani,* meaning 'Iguana,' which is a kind of lizard. Columbus named the island San Salvador, in honor of God. And because he thought he had reached the Indies, in Asia, Columbus called the people he saw 'Indians.' "

"Did the Indians attack Columbus?" one child asked.

"No," the teacher said. "The Arawak people were peaceful. They treated the Spanish explorers as friends.

"Columbus stayed on San Salvador for only a few days. He then sailed to Cuba and Hispaniola. Then, in January, Columbus sailed for Spain. He left forty men on Hispaniola to search for gold. Despite the friendliness of the Arawak, the Spaniards treated the Indians cruelly. Finally, the Arawak killed them.

"A year later, Columbus returned. After learning what happened, he started a new

*This old painting shows Columbus landing on
San Salvador. The Arawak did not really dress
at all like the Indians shown in the painting.*

colony farther down the coast. The Arawak people there also greeted the Spaniards as friends. But the Spaniards feared that what had happened before might happen again. So, they used their guns to terrify the Arawak. Columbus then ordered the Indians on this part of the island to bring the colony a large amount of gold every three months!

"By 1502, the Spanish had made slaves of all the Arawak people on Hispaniola. Every Arawak man had to serve a Spanish master for six or eight months a year, mining gold or working on a farm.

"The men were worked hard and fed very little. Many of them died of starvation or disease. Some killed themselves in despair. Many Arawak mothers even killed their sons rather than see them grow up to be slaves! By the year 1535, there were only about five hundred Arawak left on Hispaniola.

"The same thing happened to the Arawak on other islands. By 1550, there were only a few thousand Arawak left in the West Indies, most of them on Cuba. Then, the slavery was stopped. The Arawak were allowed to live in their own towns, own property, and rule themselves.

"As time went on, many of the Spanish colonists married Arawak women. They brought their children up like Spanish children. Today, the Arawak and their way of life have vanished from the West Indies."

"Aren't there any Arawak Indians at all?" asked one boy.

"Not in the West Indies," said the teacher. "The only Arawak who are left live near the Amazon River in South America."

The Aztec

City Dwellers of Mexico

The Aztec people lived in a great, broad
valley in Central Mexico. Five hundred years
ago, about one hundred thousand people lived
in the Aztec capital of Tenochtitlan (tay nohch
tee TLAHN). Tenochtitlan was built on a lake.
Today, Mexico City stands on the same
ground.

The emperor, the supreme ruler of all the
Aztec, was a noble who was chosen by the
other nobles. Most of the Aztec people had
regular, daily jobs. Many were farmers.
Others might be carpenters, housebuilders, or
metalworkers. There were also soldiers,
priests, and government officials.

The Aztec had a great civilization. They had
a kind of picture writing and knew how to
work with numbers. They built great temples
and palaces. But they borrowed many of their
ideas from the Toltec, who lived in Mexico
before them, as well as from the Maya of
Central America.

The Aztec were warlike and cruel. Their
armies conquered many of the people who
lived near them. Every year, the Aztec
sacrificed thousands of these people to the
Aztec gods.

A schoolboy of Tenochtitlan

It was the middle of the afternoon, the hottest part of the day. Spicy smells of cooking came from the houses of the city. The women were preparing the main meal of the day. From the House of the Young, the school that stood near the neighborhood temple, a crowd of boys burst forth. Their lessons over for a while, they were going home to eat.

One of the boys, Bee-in-the-Reeds, felt very proud of himself. His teacher, Fire Coyote, had praised him because he had remembered all the words of the sacred song the boys had learned that day. Not one of the other boys had done as well! In fact, one boy, who was a neighbor of Bee-in-the-Reeds, did so poorly he had been punished. His hair had been burned a little and then cut off.

As Bee-in-the-Reeds walked along slowly, he could see the great, dark, cone-shape of Popocatepetl, Smoking Mountain, in the distance. Its top was white with snow. Today, Smoking Mountain was quiet. But sometimes it rumbled loudly and poured out great, black clouds.

The narrow street ran alongside one of the city's many canals. As usual, the canal was filled with boats. As Bee-in-the-Reeds stopped to look at them, someone pushed quickly past him. He turned and saw it was the boy who had been punished at school. "Ha, ha, no hair!" Bee-in-the-Reeds yelled.

The boy hung his head in shame and

hurried on. He'd probably be punished again when he got home. His father might prick him with the thorns of a maguey plant. Or, the boy might have his head held in the bitter, choking smoke of burning chili peppers.

Bee-in-the-Reeds soon reached his house. Like the other houses nearby, it sat at the edge of seven or eight long, narrow islands that stretched out into the water. The people had made these islands by piling mud into large woven mats. Rows of poles stuck into the shallow bottom of the lake held up the edges of the mats. All of the mud in the mats came from the bottom of the lake.

Bee-in-the-Reed's father, Angry Turkey, was a farmer. On these long strips of moist, rich soil he grew corn, tomatoes, and other plants. The mud from the lake was so rich he could raise several different crops a year.

The family was ready to eat when Bee-in-the-Reeds came into the house. Everyone sat on woven mats on the floor, around the cooking fire. His little sister, Jade Doll, grinned at him as she munched on half a tortilla. His mother, Blue Corn Flower handed him a whole tortilla. He rolled it into a tube and scooped up a mouthful of beans with it.

"My teacher complimented me today," Bee-in-the-Reeds proudly told his parents. "I was the only one who knew all the words of the song to the Corn Goddess!"

"That is good," said his father. "It is important to know the songs that honor the gods. And are you learning to use your weapons well?"

"I am getting better," answered Bee-in-the-

Reeds, his mouth full of food. "Fire Coyote says so."

"Work hard at it," his father told him. "When you grow up and become a warrior, I want you to take an enemy prisoner. That is what I did when I was a warrior. We need many prisoners so that we can sacrifice them to the gods."

Bee-in-the-Reeds finished his tortilla. But, because he was eleven years old, he was allowed to have half of another tortilla. He scooped up as many beans as he could with it, and crammed it into his mouth.

"Do not put it all into your mouth at once!" his mother scolded.

Bee-in-the-Reeds took a long drink of water. The meal was now over. If his family had been wealthy, or nobles, they would all take a long nap. But common people had no time for such luxury. They had too much work to do.

Bee-in-the-Reeds spent the rest of the day helping his father and learning from him. Jade Doll, who was only four, helped her mother around the house, learning from her. By the time Jade Doll was sixteen, she would know how to cook, make thread, weave cloth, and care for a house. She would be ready to marry a young man picked by her parents.

At the age of fifteen, Bee-in-the-Reeds would spend most of his time at school. He would even sleep there at night. He would be taught to be a soldier and would fight in battles. In time, his parents would pick a girl for him to marry. Then, he would probably become a farmer, like his father.

But, if he were a very good soldier and took many prisoners, Bee-in-the-Reeds could become a commander. That might make him wealthy. He dreamed of becoming an Eagle Knight, in a feathered costume and eagle mask. He could wear a colorful cloak, a gold ornament in his nose, and a carved jade plug in his lower lip! Then everyone would know how brave he was!

But that was years ahead. Right now, he had to help his father plant chili peppers.

Aztec ways

The way an Aztec dressed depended upon who he was and what he did. Aztec clothes showed if someone was a worker, a high official, a brave soldier, or a rich merchant.

A farmer or worker wore only a breechclout of rough white cloth made from plant leaves. His wife wore a plain white skirt that reached to her ankles, and a kind of shirt. Children dressed like their parents—boys in breechclouts and girls in long skirts. Working men, women, and children went barefoot.

A wealthy Aztec, such as a merchant, dressed a bit differently. A man still wore a breechclout, but it was made of cotton. It was often decorated with designs. He also wore a cloak of white cotton, tied over his shoulder.

Wealthy people usually wore sandals made of woven plant leaves or leather.

Noblemen and very rich men wore cloaks that were dyed bright colors and decorated with designs. A rich man with many cloaks might wear several at a time, one on top of another. This showed how wealthy he was.

The way a soldier dressed showed how brave he was. Soldiers who were especially brave could become Jaguar Knights or Eagle Knights. A Jaguar Knight wore the skin of a jaguar, with the jaguar's head over his own. An Eagle Knight wore a feathered costume and a helmet shaped like the head of an eagle with an open beak.

A common soldier usually wore sandals, a breechclout, and a sort of short-sleeved shirt that reached to his knees. If he had never captured a prisoner in battle, he kept his head

There was rejoicing when Aztec soldiers brought in prisoners after a battle. The prisoners would be sacrificed to the Aztec gods. But, strange as it may seem, the prisoners were proud and willing to be sacrificed! They believed that they would then go straight to a beautiful heaven.

The Aztec often wore lip decorations such as the gold serpent, above. The decoration fitted through a hole made in the skin below a person's lip.

shaved, except for a clump of hair at the back. But a man who had captured an enemy could wear long hair and a decorated cloak. A man who had taken several prisoners could also wear special ear and lip ornaments and other decorations.

The Aztec wore many kinds of jewelry. Rich people wore golden necklaces, armbands, ear decorations, and gold or jade rods through their nose or lower lip. Poor people wore ornaments of stone or sea shell.

Of course, the most beautifully dressed of all the Aztec was the emperor. He had cloaks made of white duck feathers, of coyote fur, and of many different colors of cloth. His cloth cloaks were trimmed with feathers and decorated with designs. Only the emperor could wear a nose ornament made of the greenish-blue stone we call turquoise. And only the emperor was allowed to wear a turquoise-colored cloak.

The house of an Aztec worker or farmer was a one-room hut, shaped like a rectangle. It had a low doorway, but no windows. The floor was just the ground. Some houses were made of dried clay bricks. Others were made of poles and plant stems woven together and smeared with wet clay. The clay dried into a hard plaster. Most houses had slanted roofs made of dried plant leaves.

On the floor would be a few woven mats for sitting on and sleeping on. One or two wooden chests held clothes and other belongings. Baskets, cooking pots, and other things used every day were piled against the walls. There would be several statues of gods, made of wood, stone, or clay. A cage made of dried, woven plant leaves might hang from a wall. This was for the family's pet parrot.

In the middle of the floor was the "stove." It was a round, flat plate made of dried clay. It sat on three large stones. A fire was built under it. It was used for cooking tortillas and other kinds of food.

The house of a wealthy Aztec was often a small palace. It might have a dining room, a kitchen, separate rooms for each member of the family, rooms for servants, storerooms, and a large room for entertaining. The walls were made of stone or clay, covered with plaster. The doorway of each room was often covered with a cloth curtain.

The floor of such a house was made of a sort of cement. The roof, made of rows of logs covered with plaster, was flat. Many wealthy Aztec covered their roofs with earth and planted gardens on them.

Several special rooms in the house had no roof. These rooms were like little inside yards. The doors of most of the other rooms opened onto one of these yards. People would often sit in a yard, under an awning.

The Aztec emperor and many wealthy

An Aztec artist made this stone carving of a grasshopper.

nobles had two-story houses. These houses had large rooms and yards. But even rich people didn't have much more furniture.

Have you ever eaten a tamale (tuh MAH lee) or a tortilla (tohr TEE yuh)? A tortilla is a thin, flat, crisp pancake made of corn meal mixed with water. A tamale is a thick, mushy, corn-meal pancake. It's spread with a thick

Every Aztec city and town had a market place. There, shoppers bought food, clothes, and other things. For money, the Aztec used gold dust, copper axes, and cocoa beans.

coat of cooked meat or vegetables, then rolled up. These foods came to us from the Aztec. Women bought ears of dried corn and ground the kernels into coarse powder, or meal for tamales, tortillas, and other foods.

Aztec workers ate breakfast at about ten o'clock. This was usually just a bowl of corn-meal mixed with water—a sort of mushy pudding. The main meal was eaten in the middle of the afternoon. At this meal, people usually had something such as tortillas and beans in a spicy sauce.

People used the tortillas as spoons. They rolled them up and dipped them into the beans. A five- or six-year-old could have one tortilla at a meal. A twelve- or thirteen-year-old was allowed to eat two.

Most Aztec never ate much meat. They couldn't afford it. But for a special occasion, they might buy a turkey or a small dog at the market.

The emperor and nobles had more and better food than workers. They ate such things as stewed ducks, fish in a sauce of tomatoes and chili peppers, and other tasty dishes. With their meals, they drank a frothy drink made of whipped chocolate flavored with honey or vanilla.

Quetzalcoatl

Coatlique

Aztec gods

The Aztec believed that a god or goddess controlled the sun, rain, wind, flowers, fire, and so on. And so, they had dozens of gods and goddesses to worship.

One of the most important gods to the Aztec was Quetzalcoatl (keht sahl koh AH t'l), god of life and learning, who had created the human race. Another important god was Huitzilopochtli (wee tse loh POHCH tlee), god of the sun and of war.

The Aztec thought that these two gods, and many others, looked like humans. But other gods and goddesses, such as Coatlique (koh aht LEE kway), the earth goddess, were horrible monsters.

Huitzilopochtli

The tale of Jappan

An Aztec legend

There was once a man called Jappan who wanted to become the favorite of the gods. To do this, he knew he would have to show the gods that he was worthy.

Jappan left his home, his wife, and all his belongings and went out into the desert. He searched until he found a high rock. With great difficulty, he climbed to the top. Then he promised to stay on the rock forever. He would never come down, not even to talk to another person.

The gods decided to test Jappan. They sent the demon Yaotl (yah OH t'l) to spy on him. If Jappan did not keep his word, Yaotl was to punish him.

Yaotl watched Jappan for a long time. Not once did Jappan break his word. The demon grew angry, for he hated humans. He did not want to see one of them become the favorite of the gods. He decided to try to force Jappan to break his word.

So, Yaotl sent many beautiful girls, one after the other, to the rock. Each girl stood at the foot of the rock and begged Jappan to come down and talk to her. But Jappan paid no attention to any of them.

Tlazolteotl (tlah zohl tay OH t'l), the goddess of love and beauty, watched all this. It angered her that Jappan was impolite to so many beautiful girls. So she went to the rock herself, to see if she could make him come down.

"Dear Jappan," she said in a sweet voice,

"I am Tlazolteotl. I think it is good that you
have kept your word all this time. I can see
how hard it must be. I would like to help you.
Will you come down and help me climb up the
rock so that we can talk.

Poor Jappan did not realize that it was a
trick. He thought he must now be the
favorite of the gods. Besides, Tlazolteotl was
very beautiful. He just couldn't resist her. So
he climbed down from the rock.

Instantly Yaotl appeared, waving a knife.
"Foolish one, you have broken your word," he
gloated. "Now I shall cut off your head!"

"No, no," cried Jappan, trying to run away.
"It's not fair! I was tricked!"

Jappan couldn't escape the demon. Yaotl caught hold of him and cut off his head. But the gods, who were watching, did not think Jappan should die. They only wanted him to be punished. So they brought Jappan back to life—but not as a human. They turned him into the first scorpion. Jappan was so ashamed at having broken his word that he hid under the rock. And this is what all scorpions have done ever since.

Yaotl had hurried off to find Jappan's wife, Tlahuitzin (tlah HOO it zihn). He seized her and brought her to the rock.

"Your foolish husband broke his word and was punished," cried Yaotl. Then he cut off her head, as he had cut off Jappan's.

At once, the gods brought her back to life as a scorpion. She joined her husband under the rock. After a time, they had many scorpion children. They can be seen in the desert to this day.

The gods felt that a great wrong had been done. They had told Yaotl to punish Jappan. But they had not expected Yaotl to kill him. And they felt that Yaotl had no right at all to kill Tlahuitzin. So to punish Yaotl, they changed him into a grasshopper and left him by the rock. When the scorpions saw the grasshopper, they began to chase him. And Jappan's family still chases Yaotl whenever they see him.

248

The end of an empire

"My brother is a student at the University of Mexico," Consuela told her friend, Ramon. "He's studying about the Aztec. Some of our ancestors were Aztec."

"All of my ancestors were Spanish—I think." Ramon declared.

Consuela giggled. "Lots of mine were, too. It's funny, because at first, the Spaniards and Aztec fought each other!

"My brother says the first Spanish explorers came to Mexico in 1517. They found gold ornaments in some of the villages. Soon, other explorers came, looking for gold. In 1519, Hernando Cortés landed in Mexico with six hundred men. Cortés heard of the great

This old Aztec drawing shows the Aztec emperor Montezuma (seated, left) meeting with the Spanish explorer Cortés. Behind Cortés is an Indian woman who spoke the Aztec and Spanish languages. She helped the Spaniards and the Aztec talk together.

Aztec city of Tenochtitlan. He was sure he would find gold there.

"When the Spaniards got to Tenochtitlan, the Aztec emperor, Montezuma, greeted them with gifts. He realized the Spaniards were too powerful to fight. He hoped to prevent bloodshed. But the Spaniards, fearful because they were so few, seized Montezuma and made him their prisoner.

"The Spaniards ruled the city for about eight months. Then, while Cortés was away, the Aztec revolted. The Spaniards had to fight their way to safety. Montezuma was killed. So were many Spaniards.

"Cortés soon got more soldiers. And thousands of the people the Aztec had conquered joined him. With this big army, Cortés attacked Tenochtitlan.

"For several months there was terrible fighting. The Aztec defended their city bravely. But the armor and weapons of the Spaniards were too much for the Aztec. Many thousands of them were killed. Finally, they had to give up.

"That was the end of the Aztec empire. The Spaniards destroyed Tenochtitlan and started building what is now Mexico City. The Aztec had to obey Spanish laws and live as ordered by the Spaniards. Many Aztec were forced to work for the Spaniards, almost as slaves. But after a time, Spaniards and Aztec married one another. They became one people—Mexicans.

"Many of the people in small villages near Mexico City are part Aztec. A lot of these people still speak Nahuatl (NAH wah t'l), the Aztec language. But they live just like most other Mexicans."

The Yawalapiti

People of the Tropical Forest

The Yawalapiti lived deep in the forests of South America, in what is now the central part of Brazil. Their village was near one of the many rivers that run through the forest.

This part of the world is always warm. At certain times it is very hot and wet. From December to May, there is much rain. Sometimes, a soft rain falls steadily for days at a time. But there are also cloudbursts that cause terrible floods. Then, for the next five months there is hardly any rain at all.

This land is the home of many kinds of animals—jaguars, monkeys, tapirs, and brightly colored birds. The rivers are filled with fish. One kind, the sharp-toothed piranha, is more dangerous than a shark.

The Yawalapiti hunted, fished, gathered wild foods, and raised a few kinds of crops. They were led by a chief. When he died, a son, nephew, or son-in-law became chief.

A number of other small tribes lived near the Yawalapiti. These tribes were like the Yawalapiti in most ways. Often, the tribes traded with one another. But, just as often, they fought and raided each other. They even stole women and children.

The fish-catching day

It was dawn. As usual, the forest was full
of waking-up sounds. Monkeys began to
shriek and whistle. A curassow, perched on a
tree limb, squawked loudly. Somewhere near
the river, a jaguar roared.

The boy woke up. He blinked, yawned, then
bounced out of his hammock. The whole
village would soon be up and getting ready.
This was a special morning—a fish-catching
morning!

Of course, men often went fishing. They
shot fish with arrows or speared them. But
today's fishing would be different. The whole
village would help. For this was the season
when many fish could be caught at once. It
was done in a special way—with poison made
from vines.

Yesterday, some of the young men had
trooped past the clearing where the corn and
manioc were planted. They had gone on into
the forest. There, among the branches of
many of the trees hung the special vines that
were needed.

These vines were thick as a person's arm.
They twined and coiled like snakes through
the branches of the trees. Some of the young
men hacked through the vines with saws
made from the jaws of a fish called a piranha.
It was hard work. When a vine had been cut
through, other young men yanked and
twisted and tugged until the vine fell to the
ground. And after that, the men cut the vines
into arm-length pieces.

These pieces now lay waiting to be cut up.
The boy would help chop the vines, but first

he wanted to feed his parrot. He took part of an ear of corn from where he had tucked it into his hammock. The parrot was perched on a stick the boy had stuck into the grass-covered wall of the house.

The parrot was very young. The boy had found it alone in a nest only a few days before. It couldn't eat hard corn yet. So, the boy chewed some of the kernels until they were soft. Then he gave these to the bird.

"Come on, let's go!"

Some of the other boys, carrying stone axes, called to him. They were already starting toward the forest. With one finger, the boy gently stroked the parrot's head for a moment. Then he ran to join the others.

The forest soon echoed with the sound of chopping. The boy knelt over a piece of vine and pounded as hard as he could. Slowly, it broke into thin, golden-yellow strips.

Soon, the boys heard talking and laughter. The men of the village were coming through the forest to where the boys were working. The men tied the golden strips of vine into bundles. They lifted these to their shoulders. Carrying the bundles, they made their way to the river.

The men went to a special place where the river swelled out, forming a tiny lake. Where the lake joined the river, it was very narrow. And at this season, when no rain had fallen for many months, the water was low. Some of the men had built a fence of branches across the narrow part. Now, all the fish in the tiny lake were trapped!

Shouting loudly, the men jumped into the water with the vines! Wading back and forth,

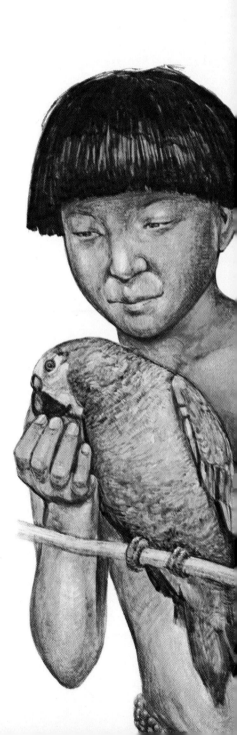

they held the vines in the water. They pounded them with clubs. Splat! Splat!

As the men beat the bundles, bluish sap from the vines began to flow into the water. Slowly, the bluish sap spread out. After a time, the men left the water.

Fish began to float to the surface. First one, then several, then dozens of fish! They floated with their white bellies upward. The lake was dotted with floating fish. The vine sap, spreading through the water, had poisoned them!

About noontime, everyone in the village went to the lake. With the women and other children, the boy dashed into the shallow water. He scooped up one fish after another, dumping them into the basket he carried. When the basket was full, the boy waded ashore and dumped the fish onto the grass. Then he went back for more.

Some of the larger fish had not been put to sleep by the poison. But they were dazed. They swam slowly and were easily caught. When a man saw one of these fish, he just jabbed an arrow into it and lifted it out of the water.

Soon there were many piles of fish on the bank. Plenty for every family! In a little while, fish would be roasting on grills throughout the village. Tonight, after everyone had eaten, the men would dance and shake their turtle-shell rattles. And the women would sing.

It had been a good fish-catching day!

Yawalapiti children twisted leaves around ears of corn to make bird and animal shapes. The corn was then hung in houses, to use as food when needed.

Yawalapiti children also made a flying toy. They tied two insects together with a long string. When the insects flew, the string made shapes in the air.

Yawalapiti ways

A Yawalapiti house looked a lot like a huge haystack. It was a wide, dome-shaped frame of poles covered with bundles of dried grass. There was a low doorway on each side. A hole in the roof let out the smoke from cooking fires.

Several related families shared each house. Each family had its own space where they cooked, ate, and slept. The people slept in hammocks made of twisted cotton and plant leaves. The hammocks were hung between the wall and poles in the middle of the floor.

The Yawalapiti decorated their houses with ears of dried corn. They twisted the leaves of each ear of corn into the shape of a bird or animal. Then they hung the corn from the ceiling. When they needed the corn for food, the Yawalapiti took down some of their "decorations" and ground the corn into flour.

The Yawalapiti village had a special house

Yawalapiti men made special costumes and musical instruments that they used for religious ceremonies.

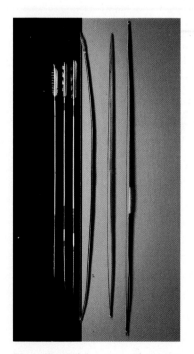

Yawalapiti bows and arrows

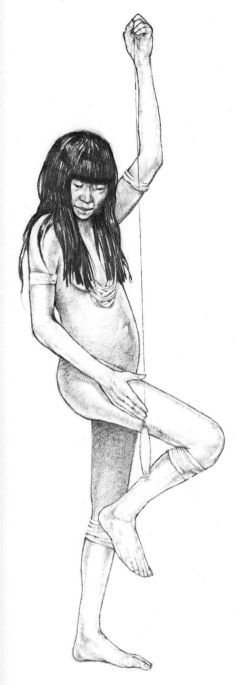

To make thread, a woman attached a wad of cotton to a cigar-shaped stone. By rubbing the cotton on her thigh, she pulled and twisted it into a long piece of thread.

that was for men only. Women weren't even allowed to peek into it. Unmarried men slept in this house at night, and it was used for all the special ceremonies and dances in which only men could take part.

In the tropical forest where the Yawalapiti lived, the weather is often steamy hot. So Yawalapiti men, women, and children simply didn't bother to wear any clothes at all. But they did decorate themselves in several ways.

Men often wore strips of woven cotton on their arms, just below the shoulder. They also wore strips of cotton on their legs, just below the knee or around the ankle. Both men and women wore necklaces made of stone beads. And both men and women often painted their bodies. Men also sometimes painted their hair.

To cut their hair, men used the sharp teeth of a piranha. The piranha is a dangerous, meat-eating fish that lives in some South American rivers.

The food the Yawalapiti ate depended on the season of the year. During the rainy season, a certain kind of fruit ripened. Women boiled the fruit. Then they put it into long containers made of bark. The containers were placed in cool water. This kept the fruit from spoiling, just as a refrigerator does. The fruit was mixed with water to make soup.

During most of the long rainy season, bread made from manioc roots was the main food. Women ground up the roots by rubbing them across a flat piece of wood with many sharp thorns stuck in it. Then the ground pulp was rolled on a rough mat to squeeze out the juice, which is poisonous. The pulp was mixed with water to make a paste.

Women spread the paste on a flat piece of hard clay over a fire to make a kind of thick pancake.

The way food was cooked depended upon who did the cooking. Boiling and baking could be done only by women. Roasting and broiling was done only by men.

Near the end of the dry season, river turtles laid millions of eggs on the riverbanks. The Yawalapiti had no trouble finding the nests and digging the eggs out of the sand. So, for a while during the dry season, roasted turtle eggs were the main food of the Yawalapiti.

The Yawalapiti decorated themselves with paint. Black paint was made by mixing charcoal with fat. Red paint was made from the berries of a plant.

Clever Frog

A Yawalapiti legend

One day, Frog found that he needed a bow. He decided to ask his brother-in-law, Jaguar, to lend him one.

As Frog walked through the village toward Jaguar's house, he met many other villagers. When they saw where he was going, they began to warn him. "If you go into Jaguar's house, he'll eat you," they said.

But Frog went into Jaguar's house anyway. "How are you, brother-in-law?" he called out.

"I'm fine," replied Jaguar, licking his lips hungrily. "Sit down and let's talk."

Frog and Jaguar sat and talked for a long time. The villagers, waiting outside to see what would happen, looked at one another. "Ah, Frog must want to be eaten," they said. "He's staying in there far too long!"

Jaguar didn't think he could get away with eating Frog with all the villagers watching his house. So he said to Frog, "Brother-in-law, why don't we go down to the river and bathe?"

Frog agreed, and they started out. As they walked, Jaguar kept trying to get behind Frog so as to pounce on him. But Frog noticed this. So he was very careful not to let his brother-in-law get behind him.

After their bath, Frog and Jaguar went back to the village. The villagers were surprised to see that Frog was still alive. "Jaguar must be getting soft," they whispered to each other. "He didn't eat Frog while they were bathing."

It was nearly dark now. Jaguar turned to Frog and said. "Brother-in-law, why don't you spend the night at my house?"

"Very well," said Frog. But before settling down for the night, Frog stepped out of the hut and caught a firefly. He opened up the firefly and took out the little lantern it carried inside itself. He rubbed the lantern over his eyelids, so that they would shine in the dark when he closed his eyes. Then Frog went back into the house, climbed into a hammock, and went to sleep.

After a while, Jaguar came slinking toward Frog's hammock. Jaguar saw Frog's eyelids shining in the dark. He thought they were Frog's eyes, wide open and looking at him. He quickly turned and crept back to his own hammock.

In the morning, Frog said, "Well, I must be going now, brother-in-law. But before I go, I want to borrow a bow and a flute."

Jaguar gave him the bow and flute. Frog then walked out into the forest. Jaguar sneaked along after him, keeping out of sight among the trees.

Frog, however, suspected that Jaguar would try to follow him. After a while, Frog came to a tribe of army ants marching across the path. He divided the ants into two groups. He sent each group into the forest, one group on each side of the path.

One group of the army ants soon found Jaguar and began to bite his feet. Jaguar stamped, trying to shake off the ants. From the sound of the stamping, Frog could tell where Jaguar was. He walked into the forest, toward him.

"Hello, brother-in-law," said Frog, softly. "Why are you following me?"

"Why, I was worried about you," Jaguar answered, trying to smile. "I was afraid that some children might harm you."

"It's not the children who want to harm me," said Frog, angrily. "It's you!"

Frog shot an arrow at Jaguar, but he missed. Jaguar dashed away through the trees. He ran through the forest until he reached the village of the Snakes.

"Frog is coming this way," he told the

Snakes. "He's a troublemaker. You ought to kill him!"

The Snakes decided to take Jaguar's advice. They hid among the trees beside the path. When Frog appeared, they leaped out. They seized him and took him back to their village.

"Wait a moment," said Frog. "I know you want to kill me. But you'd better not do it here in your village. My blood will flood the place. Kill me on the riverbank, so my blood will go into the water."

So the Snakes dragged Frog down to the river. But the instant they let go of him, he dived into the water and vanished. At once, the boa, the anaconda, and all the other Snakes jumped in after him. But they couldn't find him.

They couldn't find Frog because he swam underwater far up the river. Then he climbed out of the river and walked back toward the Snake village, singing all the way.

All the Snake warriors were still at the river, searching for Frog. There was no one in the village except the women and babies. So Frog went into all the houses and broke all the cooking pots, singing all the time!

Then Frog climbed up to the moon. He sat there, playing the flute he had borrowed from his brother-in-law, Jaguar. When Jaguar heard Frog playing the flute, he grew so angry his eyes flashed. "I told you to kill Frog," he roared at the Snakes. "But you were too stupid! Now he's up there making fun of us!"

But there was nothing they could do about it. And to this day, Frog is still playing the flute on the moon.

The shrinking forest

A young Brazilian scientist had come to the village where the Yawalapiti lived. He listened as an old man told of what had happened to the Yawalapiti since they first met white people.

"When my grandfather was a young man, almost a hundred years ago," said the old one, "he had never seen or heard of white people. Then, one day, a white man came to our part of the forest. My people began to learn about the white peoples' world.

"They saw the fine metal axes and knives that white people had. They wanted such things. Soon, some Yawalapiti men went on a long journey to find a white peoples' town. They hoped to trade for knives and axes.

"Well," the old man looked grim, "they brought some back. But they brought back something else—white peoples' sickness! White people can get well from such sickness, but we couldn't! Many people died!

"For a long time after that we didn't have much to do with white people. We lived as we always had. Then, when I was young—about thirty-five years ago—many white men came among us. They cut down great parts of the forest! They made the long, stone paths you call roads. Towns grew where there had only been trees before. The forest grew smaller! It was shrinking.

"But, there were three white men who were different. They were brothers. Their names were Orlando, Claudio, and Leonardo Villas Boas. I talked with those brothers, often. They were afraid for us. They said that if too much of the forest was taken away, the Yawalapiti and other tribes of the forest would be destroyed! This had happened in other places!

"The three brothers helped us. About twenty years ago they got the chief of your people to promise to save this part of the forest. It was made into what you call a national park. No roads or towns can be made in it. No one except the Yawalapiti and some other tribes can live here.

"And so, our home and our way of life was saved. We can still live much as our fathers and grandfathers did." The old man gave a deep sigh. "It is good. I am glad. But I wonder if it is too late? There are very few of us left. The time may come when there are no more Yawalapiti at all."

Orlando Villas Boas, shown here with an Indian mother and child, is a Brazilian. He and his brothers helped to save the forest home of the Yawalapiti and other tribes living in Brazil.

The Inca

People of the Andes Mountains

Five hundred years ago, the Inca ruled a
great empire that stretched down the west
coast of South America. This empire covered
most of what are now the nations of Peru,
Chile, and Ecuador, as well as parts of
Bolivia and Argentina.

Most of the Inca empire was in the Andes
Mountains. In this land, it is warm all year in
the valleys and cold in the mountains.

The Inca empire included many tribes that
the Inca had conquered. As many as six
million people lived in this great empire.

The people of the Inca empire were mostly
farmers. They grew different kinds of crops
in different places. They did not do much
hunting. But they did raise animals such as
llamas, guinea pigs, and ducks.

The empire was made up of many towns,
all connected by roads. The capital was the
large city of Cusco (koos koh), which still
stands in Peru.

The Inca empire was ruled by an emperor
who was worshiped as a god. Most of the
people who helped to run the empire were
also Inca. But any man who showed ability
had a chance to better himself.

Blue Egg becomes a grown-up

Blue Egg was quite hungry. She had eaten only a handful of uncooked corn yesterday. And for two days before that she had eaten nothing at all. She didn't really mind, though. She was too excited to care much about being hungry, for, those three days without food were part of a ceremony.

The ceremony would be completed today. And today was the most important day of her life up until now. Before this, she had been a little girl. But today she was to become a grown-up!

Besides not eating anything, she'd had to stay in the house for the last three days. That had been pretty boring! But it would all be over soon. In a little while, all her relatives would be outside, waiting for her. She could hear some of them outside now, talking. There would be a feast. She would be given her new grown-up name. And—she grinned excitedly at the thought—she would get presents!

As Blue Egg thought about the presents, her mother came bustling in. She was carrying a bundle of cloth. "All right," she said, smiling, "time to get ready!"

She helped Blue Egg wash. Then she slowly and carefully combed out the girl's dark, shining hair and braided it. "Do you think you can remember the new name Uncle Strong will give you today?" she joked.

"I'll remember it!" Blue Egg said, very positively. "I hope it's a pretty one."

"You will like it," her mother told her. She handed the cloth bundle to the girl. "Put these on."

Blue Egg unfolded the cloth. It was a brand-new dress. Tucked into it was a pair of new, white sandals. She wrapped the cloth tightly around herself. Her mother helped her tie the sash about her waist. Then Blue Egg slipped on the sandals. Her heart beating fast with excitement, she followed her mother through the door.

Her grandfathers, grandmothers, aunts, and uncles were all there. They smiled at her as she stepped into the sunlight. "Ai, what a beautiful lady!" called Uncle Hawk. "Why, she's as pretty as a Chosen Woman!"

Blue Egg couldn't help but grin shyly at his words. Chosen Women were picked from every village. They were the most beautiful of all the girls. They were also the best weavers of cloth.

Chosen Women were taken to the capital city of Cusco to go to school for four years. Most of the Chosen Women became the wives of great soldiers or nobles. Some became priestesses of the gods. A few might become wives of the Great Ruler himself! And a very few received the greatest honor of all—they were sacrificed to the Sun and lived happily in heaven forever!

But Blue Egg didn't think she was as pretty as a Chosen Woman. She'd had a chance to be picked several years ago. At that time, the Ruler's official had come to the village to choose from among the girls her age. But, like most of the girls, she had become a Left Out One—a girl who hadn't

been chosen. She would grow up in the village, get married, and spend the rest of her life there.

Uncle Strong walked forward and stood in front of her, smiling. "For the first two years of your life you had no name," he said. "Everyone just called you Baby. Then, there was a ceremony, like this one. Your hair was cut and you were given your child-name, Blue Egg. But today I give you the name that will be yours for the rest of your life. I name you—Star."

Star. She loved it!

Then came the presents. From Uncle Strong she got a copper pin to hold her cloak together. Uncle Hawk and his wife gave her a beautiful necklace made of shells. She also got her own comb, made of a row of thorns tied between two strips of wood. The last gift was a piece of brightly colored cloth to wear on her head on festival days.

After that it was time to eat. And Star was certainly ready for food! The pots were placed on cloths that had been spread on the ground. Then everyone sat down. The men sat in a small circle, facing one another. The women sat outside the circle, their backs to the men. They talked and laughed.

Star's way of life, and that of her family, was the same as for all the common people in the Inca empire. Except for girls who became Chosen Women, people usually spent their whole life in the village where they were born.

People spent most of their time working in the fields. But they did not really think of this as *work*. It was more like a festival or a ceremony. The people sang, danced, and played music as they planted or harvested. At other times, people worked at making cloth, pots, baskets, and wooden bowls. Even this was not really work. They made these things because they needed them.

The people in an Inca village felt safe. There was seldom any sort of trouble. And they almost always had enough to eat. The Inca were content with the life they led.

Inca ways

Inca farmers kept flocks of little woolly animals called alpacas. Most Inca clothing was made of cloth woven from the smooth, silky alpaca wool. The wool was usually dyed a color. Women, often helped by old men, twisted the wool into thread and wove the thread into cloth.

An Inca woman wore leather sandals and an ankle-length dress made of alpaca wool. On a cold day or chilly night, she usually wrapped a cloak, much like a large shawl, around her shoulders. This was held together in front by a large pin made of copper, gold, or silver.

An Inca man wore a cloth breechclout and a sort of floppy, sleeveless shirt that reached to his knees. Under his right arm, hanging from a strap over his left shoulder, was a small, square "purse." In this he kept such things as small tools, a magical charm, and a wad of coca plant leaves, which the Inca were fond of chewing.

A man often wore a large shawl just like the one worn by women. But he usually tied

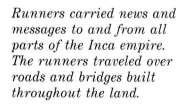

Runners carried news and messages to and from all parts of the Inca empire. The runners traveled over roads and bridges built throughout the land.

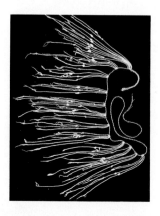

The Inca did not have writing. To keep a record of anything, they used a bundle of knotted strings called a quipu (KEE poo). The knots stood for numbers. The colors stood for the things counted.

An Inca farm house had
walls made of stones or
clay bricks covered with
clay plaster. The roof was
made of dried, woven grass.

The Inca raised llamas for
carrying things. They
also ate young llamas.

Freeze-dried potatoes were an important food. The Inca spread potatoes out to freeze on a cold night. Next day, people stamped on them to squeeze out the water. Then they were dried in the sun. They would keep for months.

the ends over his chest instead of fastening them with a pin. Men also wore sandals.

The emperor's clothing wasn't much different from what the farmers and workers wore. However, it was made of different material. Only the emperor could wear cloth made from the wool of the wild animal called a vicuna (vih KOON yuh). Special hunts were held to capture vicunas. Their wool was cut off, then they were set free.

The emperor's wives and women servants wove the vicuna wool into cloth and made all the emperor's clothes. It probably took them a long time to make each garment. Even so, the emperor never wore anything more than once! After he took a piece of clothing off, it was burned. Then the ashes were scattered so that no one else could ever touch anything the emperor had worn!

The family of an Inca farmer or worker got up at sunrise. At this hour, they usually had just a bowl of a sort of beer made from the juice of mashed-up corn. The family had its first real meal at about eight or nine o'clock in the morning. The main meal was at four or five in the afternoon.

The Inca grew a great many of the plants we also raise for food. They grew many kinds of corn, potatoes, and several kinds of grain. They also raised tomatoes, lima beans, peanuts, chili peppers, pumpkins, squashes, avocados, melons, and other plants. Inca farmers actually grew far more food than was needed. A lot of it was dried and stored away. Some of it was even burned as a sacrifice to the Inca gods.

For meat, most Inca families kept tame

guinea pigs in their house. These little
animals were fed leftovers and green plants
to make them fat. Some families also raised
ducks. People sometimes ate the meat of
llamas, the little animals the Inca used as
beasts of burden. Inca boys also hunted birds
for food, killing them with slings.

Inca women cooked the family food by
either boiling or roasting it. Cooking was
done on a kind of stove. This was a box made
of hard clay with several holes in the top. The
fire was made inside the box. Pots holding the
food to be cooked were put over the holes.
The women made soups and stews flavored
with chili peppers and spices. Corn was made
into bread, dumplings, and popcorn.

Most Inca ate off flat plates made of baked
clay. They drank from cups made of clay or
wood. But the emperor and the nobles had
gold or silver cups.

A man living in a village built his own
house with the help of his relatives. It was a
one-room house, shaped like a rectangle. The
doorway was just a rectangle-shaped opening
covered with a cloth. Because there were
usually no windows, and no hole in the roof
to let out smoke, the house was almost
always dark and smoky. But the Inca were
outdoors most of the time anyway, so they
didn't care.

Except for the stove there was no furniture
in the house. People hung their cloaks and
extra clothes on pegs on the walls. Pots and
dishes were stored against the walls. The
floor was just the bare ground. The family
slept on the floor, on llama skins or blankets
made of llama wool.

Inca cities were very different from the villages. There were big buildings and temples made of huge stone blocks. A city such as Cusco even had streets paved with stone blocks. Most city buildings were planned and built by men we would now call architects (AHR kuh tehkts)—people specially trained and skilled at building.

Near every city there stood a great stone fort. In case of attack, people took their weapons and rushed to the fort to defend themselves against the enemy.

Inca builders had only stone hammers and bronze chisels. But they were able to cut and smooth huge stone blocks and fit them together so well a pin couldn't be pushed between them. Many Inca buildings still stand.

An Inca panpipe

The Inca enjoyed music. They made one kind of musical instrument by fastening together several wooden tubes of different lengths. Blowing into each tube made a different note. We call this instrument a panpipe.

You can make a "pretend" panpipe that's easy to play. Just follow these instructions.

Materials:
- construction paper
- magic markers
- paper clips (2)
- pencil, sharp
- rubber bands (4)
- scissors
- transparent tape
- waxed paper

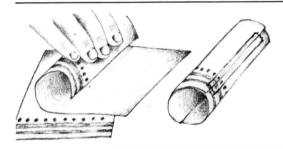

Cut construction paper into three rectangles, each a different size. Use magic markers or crayons to decorate one side of each rectangle. Roll up each rectangle to make tubes of different lengths. Tape each tube closed, as shown.

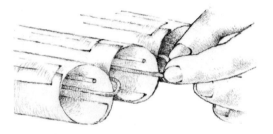

Cover one end of each tube with a piece of waxed paper held in place with a small rubber band. Use paper clips to fasten the tubes at the open ends, as shown. The open ends should all line up. Stretch the large rubber band around all three tubes to hold them together.

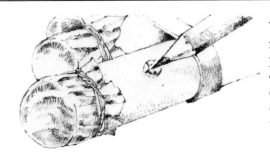

With the pencil point, punch a hole in the middle of each tube. To play your panpipes, hum loudly into the open ends of the tubes. Keep your mouth slightly open. When the holes in the tubes are open, the waxed paper will buzz. Covering the holes changes the sound.

The sacred legend of the Inca

An Inca legend

Not far from the City of the Promised
Land, there stands a mountain that is known
as the Place of the Beginning. And, once
upon a time, long ago, eight people came out
of a dark cave in that mountain.

Four of the people were brave, handsome
men. They were dressed in colorful feather
coats. In their ears they wore circles of gold.
On their arms they had golden bracelets.
These men were brothers. Their names were
Salt, Chili Pepper, Warrior, and Chief.

The other four people were beautiful
women. They wore dresses of finely woven
llama wool. These women were the sisters
and wives of the four brothers.

These eight people were the children of the
Sun. He had sent them to take command of
the world. They carried with them a golden
staff with which to test the earth for the
right place to build a city. Wherever they
stopped, they were to push the staff into the
ground. They were to do this until the staff
stuck in the ground and could not be pulled
out. On that place they were to build a city.

The eight children of the Sun started down
the mountainside. As they went, the eldest
brother, Salt, began to change the face of the
earth. He hurled great rocks about, making
deep valleys where none had been before. He
broke boulders loose and sent them tumbling
down the mountain.

The other brothers and sisters were afraid that Salt would damage the earth. So, among themselves, they agreed to get rid of him. Salt's brothers then said that some golden cups and some seeds had been left behind in the cave. They asked Salt to go back to the cave with them to get these things.

When they reached the cave, Salt went in to get the golden cups and the seeds. While he was in the cave, his brothers quickly blocked up the entrance with huge boulders. Salt roared and pushed and struggled, but it was no use. He was trapped within the cave. And there he has stayed to this day!

The brothers and sisters then held a council. They decided that each of the men should do a special thing for the good of the people who would be descended from them.

Chili Pepper changed himself into a
creature with great glowing wings. He flew
up above the others and began to speak of
the future. He revealed that his sisters and
one of his brothers would go down into the
valley beyond the mountain. There, they
would build the City of the Promised Land.
And that city, said Chili Pepper, would
become the capital of a great empire.

"As for me," he cried, "I will stay here. I
will become a stone idol for our children. Let
the boys come to me to learn how to become
men and warriors." Then Chili Pepper turned
himself into a great stone that sat forever
after upon the mountain.

The other two brothers and the four sisters
went on. They stopped for a time in a broad,
beautiful meadow. There, they planted
potatoes. It was at this place that the third
brother, Warrior, turned himself into a great
stone. This stone still sits in the meadow,
guarding the fields.

After a time, the last brother, Chief, and

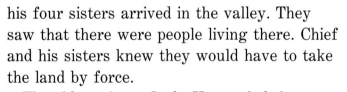

his four sisters arrived in the valley. They
saw that there were people living there. Chief
and his sisters knew they would have to take
the land by force.

The eldest sister, Lady Huaco, led the
attack. She crept up upon a man and killed
him. From his body she made a terrifying
mask. Putting on the mask, she led the others
against the people of the valley. The mask so
frightened the people that they fled from the
valley. They did not stop running until they
came to the distant mountains!

In the valley, near the river that is called
the River of Bones, Chief thrust the golden
staff into the earth. It stuck fast! This was
the place where they were to build the City of
the Promised Land.

Chief and his sisters now planted corn that
they had brought with them from the cave in
the Place of the Beginning. Nearby, they
built a house. This is how Chief and his four
sisters became the first of the people known
forever after as the Great Ones.

This wall in Cusco, Peru, was built by the Inca centuries ago. Many things the Inca built are still standing today.

The fall of the Inca

A young priest and his visitor, a tourist, sat together on a bench outside the church.

"Yes, I was born and grew up in Peru," the priest said. "In fact, right in this village. These people are my people. We are all descendants of the Inca."

He smiled. "I didn't know anything of my ancestors until I studied to be a priest. Then I learned about the Inca as a hobby. In many ways they were a great people."

"The Spaniards reached the edge of the Inca empire about 1531. There were less than two hundred of them, under the command of Francisco Pizarro. Excited by tales of immense riches, they began to move toward the Inca capital.

"They reached the city of Cajamarca in 1532. The Inca emperor, Atahualpa, was nearby with an army. He planned to trap the Spaniards in the city. But the Spaniards made a surprise attack. They opened fire with their cannons and then charged the terrified Inca soldiers. Pizarro seized the emperor and made him a prisoner.

"Atahualpa offered the Spaniards a huge treasure of gold and silver if they would set him free. They agreed. But after they got the treasure, they put the emperor to death.

"The Inca chose a new emperor. He formed a great army and tried to drive the Spaniards away. But Pizarro and his soldiers crushed the Inca. The empire fell apart. The Spaniards ruled all the Inca lands.

"Soon, many people came from Spain to make new homes here. They treated the Inca and other Indians like slaves! They took their land. They put the Indians to work in mines, digging gold and silver. And they forced them to give up their religion.

"In the hundreds of years that followed, things did get a little better for the Indians. Spanish men married Indian women. In time, many people were of mixed Spanish and Indian blood. They didn't think of themselves as Spaniards—and they didn't like being ruled by Spain. In the 1800's, Peru, Bolivia, and Ecuador fought wars against Spain, and became free nations.

"Today, there are about six million of us who are descendants of the Inca. We still speak Quechua (KEHCH wah), the Inca language. Most of my people are farmers and llama herders. They live in little villages, like this one. Here, we still have some of our own customs and way of life."

Indians Today

The ways of life of the American Indians of hundreds of years ago are gone forever. Today's Indians live in a world that is very different from the one their ancestors knew.

But to many Indians, the old ways still seem best. They try to live as their ancestors lived. As much as possible, they try to keep apart from the modern world around them.

For other Indians, today's world seems best. They are proud to be Indians, but they want to live in the same way most other people live. They don't want to be thought of as "different."

And still other Indians—many of them— try to mix the old ways and new ways. They want to keep many of their old customs and ways of life. But they also want to take advantage of the science and technology of the modern world.

Today's Indians have many problems. Some are terribly poor. Some are angry at the way they have been treated. Many feel they are at a crossroad—and they are not sure which way to go.

Many Indians live on reservations—land the government has set aside for them. Often, these are places where their people have lived for hundreds of years. But other Indians make their homes in towns and cities everywhere.

Navajo Indian boy on a reservation in Arizona

Indian children in the city of Chicago

This Apache Indian works as a lumberjack.

Indians do all kinds of work. Many are farmers, sheep or cattle herders, fishermen, or lumberjacks. Others are factory workers, or builders. Some are doctors, lawyers, scientists, teachers, and entertainers.

Maria Tallchief, who is part Osage Indian, is a famous ballet dancer. She is shown here directing a ballet rehearsal.

These Indians went to Washington, D.C., to argue for what their people want.

Many Indians believe the government has often treated them unfairly. They say that promises have been made and then broken. Many tribes now have their own tribal councils to direct the activities of the tribe and to represent it in dealings with the government. And some Indians are now demanding that old promises made to their people should be kept.

Many Indian tribes have their own government.

For most Indians, the past is precious. They are trying to keep their language, their dances and music, and a great many of the ways of their ancestors.

A Mescalero Apache performs an old dance.

These Indian children in Chicago are learning the Winnebago language.

A Cree woman making snowshoes.

There are many ways of life among Indians today. Some live in fine houses, some in sad little shacks. Some are well off—but many are poor. Some live much as their ancestors did, long ago. And some are very much a part of today's world.

The Indians on this reservation in Colorado live in comfortable, modern houses and have cars.

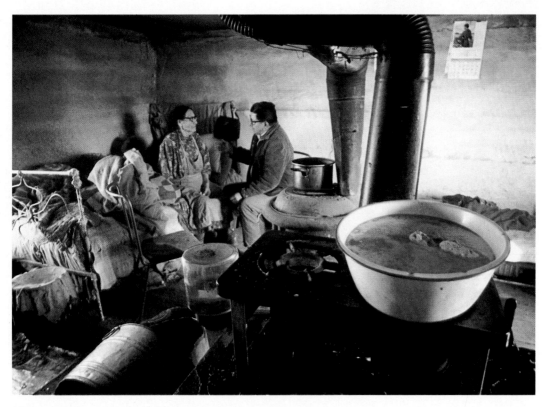

Many Indians get health care from the government.

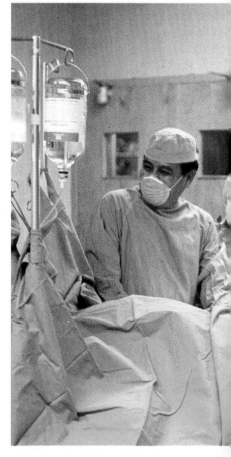

This doctor, a skilled surgeon, is the son of a Navajo medicine man.

The Tarahumara Indians of Mexico follow old ways.

Illustration acknowledgments

The publishers of *Childcraft* gratefully acknowledge the courtesy of the following photographers, agencies, and organizations for illustrations in this volume. When all the illustrations for a sequence of pages are from a single source, the inclusive page numbers are given. In all other instances, the page numbers refer to facing pages, which are considered as a single unit or spread. All illustrations are the exclusive property of the publishers of *Childcraft* unless names are marked with an asterisk (*).

Cover:	Aristocrat and Standard binding—Richard Hook; Myron Wright*; © John Running* Heritage binding—Richard Hook; Krystyna Stasiak; Jon Goodell; © John Running*; Krystyna Stasiak; © Dennis Stock, Magnum*; Field Museum of Natural History, Chicago (*Childcraft* photo); Amon Carter Museum, Fort Worth, TX*
1:	Jerry Pinkney
2–3:	Richard Hook
8–9:	Ben Manchipp
10–11:	Richard Hook; Jean Helmer
12–13:	Richard Hook
14–15:	Arizona State Museum, University of Arizona*; Richard Hook
16–17:	Kathy & Alan Linn*; Richard Hook
18–19:	Richard Hook; Shostal
20–21:	Museum of the American Indian Heye Foundation, N.Y.C.*
22–23:	Richard Hook
24–25:	© W. E. Ruth, Bruce Coleman Inc.*
26–27:	Jean Helmer; Janet LaSalle
28–29:	Ben Manchipp; Steve Liska
30–33:	Kinuko Craft
34–35:	Kinuko Craft; Michael Hampshire
36–37:	Michael Hampshire
38–39:	Michael Hampshire; Field Museum of Natural History, Chicago (*Childcraft* photo)
40–41:	*Childcraft* photo; Jean Helmer
42–43:	Ben Manchipp; Krystyna Stasiak
44–45:	Krystyna Stasiak
46–47:	Michael Kopp*
48–49:	Ben Manchipp; Steve Liska
50–51:	Richard Hook
52–53:	Richard Hook; Cranbrook Institute of Science, Bloomfield Hills, MI*
54–59:	Richard Hook
60–61:	Museum of the American Indian Heye Foundation, N.Y.C.*; *Childcraft* photo
62–63:	Field Museum of Natural History, Chicago (*Childcraft*)
64–65:	Richard Hook
66–67:	Ben Manchipp; Roberta Polfus
68–69:	Roberta Polfus
70–71:	Cranbrook Institute of Science, Bloomfield Hills, MI*; "Joseph Brant" by Charles Willson Peale, Independence National Historical Park Collection, Philadelphia*
72–73:	Ben Manchipp; Steve Liska
74–79:	Stephen Clay
80–83:	John Dawson
84–85:	Museum of the American Indian Heye Foundation, N.Y.C.*; Ben Manchipp
86–89:	Jon Goodell
90–91:	Bettman Archive*
92–93:	Frederic Remington, The Newberry Library, Chicago*
94–95:	Ben Manchipp; Steve Liska
96–99:	Kinuko Craft
100–101:	Kinuko Craft; Field Museum of Natural History, Chicago
102–103:	John Dawson; Museum of the American Indian Heye Foundation, N.Y.C.*
104–105:	John Dawson
106–107:	*Childcraft* photo; Jean Helmer
108–109:	Ben Manchipp; Krystyna Stasiak
110–113:	Krystyna Stasiak
114–115:	Loren Mozley, Dick Kent (*Childcraft* photo)
116–117:	Ben Manchipp; Steve Liska
118–123:	Kinuko Craft
124–125:	Field Museum of Natural History, Chicago
126–129:	John Dawson; Burke Memorial Washington State Museum*
130–131:	Jean Helmer; Nancy Simmerman, Atoz/Van Cleve*
132–133:	Ben Manchipp; Jon Goodell
134–135:	Jon Goodell
136–137:	Smithsonian Institution, Washington, D.C.*
138–139:	Ben Manchipp; Steve Liska
140–143:	Richard Hook
144–145:	Field Museum of Natural History, Chicago; Richard Hook
146–147:	Richard Hook; Field Museum of Natural History, Chicago
148–149:	Field Museum of Natural History, Chicago (*Childcraft* photo); Richard Hook; from *Indians and Archaeology of Missouri* by Carl H. Chapman and Eleanor F. Chapman, University of Missouri Press, © 1964 by the Curators
150–151:	Richard Hook; *Childcraft* photo; Jean Helmer
152–153:	Ben Manchipp; Roberta Polfus
154–155:	"Mohongo and Child" by Charles B. King, Collection of Dr. & Mrs. Thornton Boileau (*Childcraft* photo)
158–159:	Ben Manchipp; Steve Liska
160–163:	Kinuko Craft
164–165:	John Dawson; Museum of the American Indian Heye Foundation, N.Y.C., *Reader's Digest*; Field Museum of Natural History, Chicago (*Childcraft* photo)
166–167:	John Dawson
168–169:	Ben Manchipp; Krystyna Stasiak
170–171:	"On the Way to the Mines" published by J. M. Hutchings, The Huntington Library, San Marino, CA*
172–173:	Ben Manchipp; Steve Liska
174–175:	Richard Hook
176–177:	Richard Hook; Museum of the Cherokee Indian, Cherokee, NC, Samuel R. Spangenberg*
178–181:	Richard Hook
182–183:	Richard Hook; Field Museum of Natural History, Chicago
184–185:	*Childcraft* art; Ben Manchipp
186–189:	Dan B. Timmons
190–191:	Lehman and Duval, Philadelphia Museum of Art, given by Miss Willian Adger*; Georgia Historical Society, Savannah*
192–193:	Robert Lindneux, Woolaroc Museum, Bartlesville, OK*
194–195:	Ben Manchipp; Steve Liska
196–199:	Jerry Pinkney
200–203:	Charles McBarron
204–205:	Denver Art Museum, CO*; Charles McBarron
206–207:	*Childcraft* photo; John S. Walter; Ben Manchipp
208–209:	Jon Goodell
210–211:	"The Horse Thieves" by Charles M. Russell, Amon Carter Museum, Fort Worth, TX*
212–213:	Smithsonian Institution, Washington, DC*
214–215:	Ben Manchipp; Steve Liska
216–219:	Jerry Pinkney
220–221:	John Dawson
222–223:	John Dawson; James Teason
224–225:	John Dawson; Ben Manchipp
226–227:	Roberta Polfus
228–229:	Roberta Polfus; Field Museum of Natural History, Chicago
230–231:	"Columbus Discovering America" by Paul Kane, Joslyn Art Museum, Omaha, NE, Northern Natural Gas Collection*
232–233:	Ben Manchipp; Steve Liska
234–239:	Michael Hampshire
240–241:	Lee Boltin*; John S. Walter; Lee Boltin*
242–243:	Michael Hampshire
244–245:	George Suyeoka; Ben Manchipp
246–247:	Krystyna Stasiak
248–249:	"Lienzo di Telacala" from *Homenaje a Cristobol Colon* by Juntz Colombine de Mexico, The Newberry Library*
250–251:	Ben Manchipp; Steve Liska
252–255:	Richard Hook
256–257:	Richard Hook; A. Heiniger & M. Bisilliat*
258–259:	Richard Hook
260–261:	Ben Manchipp; Dan B. Timmons
262–263:	Dan B. Timmons
264–265:	W. Jesco von Puttkamer, © National Geographic Society*
266–267:	Ben Manchipp; Steve Liska
268–271:	Michael Hampshire
272–273:	Michael Hampshire; © Loren McIntyre, CHER*
274–275:	Michael Hampshire
276–277:	Michael Hampshire; *Childcraft* photo; Jean Helmer
278–279:	Ben Manchipp; Roberta Polfus
280–281:	Roberta Polfus
282–283:	© Loren McIntyre, CHER*
284–285:	Ben Manchipp
286–287:	© Dennis Stock, Magnum*; *Childcraft* photo
288–289:	© David Hiser*; *Childcraft* photo
290–291:	© John Running, Black Star*; © Terry & Lynn Eiler, Photo Quest*
292–293:	© David Hiser*; *Childcraft* photo; © Fred Ward, Black Star*
294–295:	© David Hiser*; © Terry & Lynn Eiler, Photo Quest*; © David Hiser*

Index

This index is an alphabetical list of the important things covered in both words and pictures in this book. The index shows you what page or pages each thing is on. For example, if you want to find out what the book tells about a particular subject, such as the Aztec, look under Aztec. You will find a group of words, called an entry, like this: **Aztec,** 232, *with picture.* This entry tells you that you can read about the Aztec on page 232. The words *with picture* tell you that there is a picture of the Aztec on this page, too. Sometimes, the book only tells you about a thing and does not show a picture. Then the words *with picture* will not be in the entry. It will look like this: **alpaca wool,** 272. Sometimes, there is only a picture of a thing in the book. Then the word *picture* will appear before the page number, like this: **bone comb,** *picture,* 60.

Cyclo-teacher® The easy-to-use learning system

Features hundreds of cycles from seven valuable learning areas

Here's how Cyclo-teacher works— in 3 easy steps!

Step 1—Asks a new question or poses a problem.

Step 2—Learner writes in answer or response.

Step 3—Learner checks his or her answer against correct response by flipping a lever.

Cyclo-teacher—the remarkable learning system based on the techniques of programmed instruction—comes right into your home to help stimulate and accelerate the learning of basic skills, concepts, and information. Housed in a specially designed file box are the Cyclo-teacher machine, Study Wheels, Answer Wheels, a Manual, a Contents and Instruction Card, and Achievement Record sheets.

Your child will find Cyclo-teacher to be a new and fascinating way to learn—much like playing a game. Only, Cyclo-teacher is much more than a game—it teaches new things

. . . reinforces learning . . . and challenges a youngster to go beyond!

Features hundreds of Study Cycles to meet the individual needs of students—your entire family—just as the *Childcraft Annual* is a valuable learning aid. And, best of all, lets you track your own progress—advance at your own pace! Cyclo-teacher is available by writing us at the address below:

The Childcraft Annual
Post Office Box 3822
Chicago, IL 60654

These beautiful bookstands—

specially designed to hold your entire program, including *Childcraft Annuals*.

Height: 26-3/8''
with 4'' legs.
Width: 28-3/4''
Depth: 8-3/16''

Height: 8-3/4''
Width: 14-1/2''
Depth: 8''

Most parents like having a convenient place to house their *Childcraft Annuals* and their *Childcraft* library. A beautiful floor-model bookstand—constructed of solid hardwood—is available in either walnut or fruitwood finish.

You might prefer the attractive hardwood table racks, also available in either walnut or fruitwood finish. Let us know by writing us at the following address:

The Childcraft Annual
Post Office Box 3822
Chicago, IL 60654